Alwyn Woolley

SOUTH FACING SLOPE

Carlo Carlisle .

SOUTH FACING SLOPE
writings from COUNTRY LIFE

CARLA CARLISLE

SNAKESHEAD
PRESS

Published by

SNAKESHEAD PRESS

Stanton, Bury St Edmunds, Suffolk, IP31 2DW, England

First published in 2001

Copyright © Carla Carlisle

The Author and Publishers are grateful to
COUNTRY LIFE for permission to reproduce
these articles.

Typeset by J L Design
Troston, Suffolk

Printed and bound in Great Britain by
St Edmundsbury Press, Suffolk

This book is printed on acid free paper

ISBN 0-9540924-0-6

www.snakesheadpress.com

CONTENTS

II FLOWERING

ACKNOWLEDGMENTS

This book would not exist if Sandy Mitchell hadn't persuaded me to write the weekly *Spectator* column on the back page of COUNTRY LIFE. I'm still amazed that he thought I could do it.

It also wouldn't exist if Anne Wright hadn't waited with faithful patience for copy that always arrived at the last minute. I am truly grateful to them both.

I believe that magazine columns are like peonies, a great bloom that is over before you know it, ephemeral creations that are not meant for the more purposeful world of acid-free paper. That's what I told Larry Ashmead who first proposed that these columns become a book. Although he didn't end up as my editor, he has become the kind of friend that every writer needs.

My organisational skills prevented me from keeping copies of all my columns. Last Christmas Nancy McLaren presented me with a beautiful binder of the complete collection. She is a generous friend.

I'm particularly indebted to Susan Dooley who took on the task of fishing out the duds. When I moaned that all the columns needed a dramatic overhaul to make them more bookish, she told me to stop tampering with them.

Francine Raymond, Christopher Jordan and Jenny Lawrence-Yeates did so many essential things I cannot even count them.

Marie Brenner, Virginia Graham, Judith Harris, Jorn Langberg, Will McLain and Valerie Wade are the friends who pushed me, soothed me, and rocked me into writing by their energy, love and wisdom.

My special thanks to Clive Aslet, editor of COUNTRY LIFE, who gave this collection his permission and his blessing.

The sunshine in these pages and in my life is Sam Carlisle. He nobly tolerated my use of his words and experiences. I hope someday he will find in these pages an honest memoir of his childhood. Maybe they will make up for the shoeboxes of photographs that still aren't in the album.

And last, and first, my eternal thanks to Kenneth who brought me to Wyken. Without him this would have been a very different story.

*For Kenneth and Sam down here
and for Red up there.*

INTRODUCTION

A few months after I began writing *The Spectator* column on the back page of COUNTRY LIFE I received a letter from a reader in New Jersey. It began: 'I did not subscribe to COUNTRY LIFE, the most English thing there is, in order to read an American.'

In those early days I didn't need a reader's letter in order to feel like a trespasser on the property of a sacred English institution. I'd send off my copy and it would re-appear with 'like' converted into 'such as', 'gas station' translated to 'petrol station'. In a column about ostriches and farm diversification I began with the line: 'I was born on the banks of the Yazoo River.' Back came an insistent editorial plea: *Can't you begin this on the fruit farm in Essex?*

But as time passed, the differences – historical, linguistic, emotional – became less troublesome. Maybe I just learned how to behave, but the English institution and I began to warm to each other.

On one of his visits to Wyken, my father complained that I was reading too much to my son, that I should 'take time to tell him stories, *your* stories'. I took his advice to heart and to the column. I told my stories, of how I got here and why I stayed. I told the stories of a Suffolk farm that goes back to Domesday as it faced the 21st century. I told about the people who have worked here all their lives – farmers, gardeners, gamekeepers – and the people who bring new life to this community: winemakers, shopkeepers, chefs.

And I wrote about my family. If my husband emerges as the most gentle and long-suffering Englishman on earth, then I got it about right. I've always liked the story about Nancy Astor returning to Virgina after her honeymoon and introducing her new husband Waldorf to her beloved Aunt Liza. 'Why, Miss Nancy,' her old nurse cried, 'you sho' done outmarried yo'self.' Southern women are incapable of thinking they have outmarried themselves but in my heart I know I did.

My (then) nine-year old son Sam had a more enterprising approach to my pen. Early on he struck a deal: if he appeared in a column he got £1. If the entire column was about him, the stakes ran higher. As he rarely bothered to scan the back page of COUNTRY LIFE, payment was on the honour system.

The most surprising thing about writing this column was the revelation that, however unique the events I described felt to me, they were typical. Whether it was the death of a beloved old dog, the departure of a too-young son to boarding school or the contracting-out of a farm for economic survival, I discovered that my feelings of sadness, exasperation, joy and bewilderment are what most people feel. We all share a longing to make sense of our lives.

I wrote these miniature essays about country life for COUNTRY LIFE as the 20th century was drawing to a close. There is an air of gloominess that hovers over the writing. We are now in the dawn of the 21st century and pale gloom has blossomed into full-blown melancholy. Carpets that have softened the footfall of three generations of Carlisles at Wyken are now soaked in disinfectant and line the entrances to the farm. Our flocks of Shetland and Jacob sheep are isolated in fields as far from the public as possible. Signs forbidding entrance to woodlands, meadows and fields fly like bunting from all our gates. The plague of Foot and Mouth hasn't reached this corner of Suffolk but we take nothing for granted.

Our ewes have produced a record crop of sturdy beautiful lambs. Confined to a single field, they have managed to make Kenneth's precious wildflower meadow look like an inner-city playground. Each evening as I take buckets of the sheep nuts they need to supplement their meagre grazing, I chew over a passage that André Gide wrote in his journal: 'Despite every resolution of optimism, melancholy occasionally wins out: man has decidedly botched up the planet.'

The Foot and Mouth crisis has also brought home to me what I loved most about writing these columns. Once a week I got to give into my troublesome urge to set the world straight.

When I told my father that I had agreed to write a weekly column, he was sceptical and wary. Two things troubled him. First he wondered whether I would be able to deliver on time. He had known me longer that anyone else on earth and he reminded me of a recent event involving my writing. While he was sitting with my sister in the car that was waiting to take us to the church for my mother's funeral, I was slumped over the dining room table writing the final paragraph of the eulogy that I'd worked on for two days. When I finally slid in beside him on the back seat, he turned to me and said in his patient drawl, 'well, this brings a whole new meaning to the word *deadline*'.

The other problem had to do with his idea of columnists in general. He was troubled by what he considered their infantile notion that everything that happened to them was of genuine and general interest.

'Take the job if you want it,' he advised, 'but put a time limit on it.' He was convinced that columns were a flimsy business, that they bred conceit in writers.

The weekly deadline was like bringing a pit bull terrier into the home. It was always there, thrashing, snarling, gnawing at me. On a good week I would feel mild panic as the Wednesday afternoon deadline closed in; on a bad week I felt insane. I would sit in front of my Apple Mac convinced I'd had a stroke, too mild to be detected by my family but my readers would instantly perceive that my mind was shot. When one kind reader wrote that my column reads 'like you love writing', I could only reply guiltily: Nope, what I love is *having written.*

As for my father's second worry, I hoped that I'd bypassed that one by setting a time limit of three years. But as I was writing this introduction, I swear I heard his slow baritone saying, 'A *collection* of columns? Sugar, don't you think that constitutes an act of conceit?'

What can I say? Of course he's right.

Carla Carlisle

Wyken
June 2001

I
Bud Burst

PATRIOTIC NERVE

A MAGNIFICENT ancient English oak tree presides over us here at Wyken. One summer evening a few days after our honeymoon, my husband told me: 'Just think, that tree is older than America.' I felt respectful awe, until I repeated it to my father. 'Sugar,' he said, in his lazy Southern voice, 'there are heaps of trees in America older than America.'

Alistair Cooke is like one of those trees. His *Letter from America* began before I was born but I heard it only when I came to England. These letters are like an anchor and a touchstone. They make me homesick, proud and wiser. They also feel addressed to me personally. That is Mr Cooke's great art.

Some evenings, I try to give Sam a seven-year-old's version of *Letter from America*. It's not easy. His heroes are all English: Robin Hood, King Arthur and Richard Hannay. Paul Revere and Patrick Henry don't really excite him in the same way. But he does like the music. We sing *Amazing Grace,* the best American song ever written by an Englishman. We sing Otis Redding songs, hymns, freedom songs and Elvis Presley.

Last night he requested something new. I sang *God Save the Queen* which always moves me, although *My Country, 'Tis of Thee* to the same tune does not. I'm like Maude in the film *Harold and Maude* who says 'I don't believe in monarchy but I miss the kings and queens'.

'Sing that again,' begs Sam. I ask him to sing with me but he claims he doesn't know it.

'Don't you ever sing it at school?' I ask.

'Nope, I've never heard it before.'

After he's asleep I go downstairs and look in a BBC schools songbook and find headings for the *Created World*, the *Human Family*, *Seasons*, *Harvest* – but no *England*, no *Britain*, no *My Country*.

We were brought up real little patriots. Everything we saw touched our American soul: buffalo nickels, the Statue of Liberty, bald eagles. Every morning in our classrooms, under the dreamy gaze of George Washington in a cloud, we pledged allegiance to the flag and to the Republic for which it stood, 'one nation, under God, with liberty and justice for all'. Hand over heart. I could list a thousand things, such as drive-by shootings, Walmarts, Quentin Tarantino and Patrick Buchanan, that get on my patriotic nerve. But when the Fourth of July and Thanksgiving roll round, Americans gratefully celebrate being American.

Do the English ever celebrate being English? The Scots, the Welsh, the Irish all feel intense pride, but the English have convinced themselves that patriotic feeling is intellectually suspect. Somehow in England, the brainier you are, the less able you are to love your country.

Sam is half-English. I want him to know something about the goodness, amiability and civilised manners and morals that made England. I'm aware of England's misdeeds and defects – I'm the daughter of a fervent disciple of Thomas Paine – but I also share the belief that English and American civilisations are based on the same fundamental ideas and outlook.

Meanwhile, I will teach Sam *Battle Hymn of the Republic* and *God Save the Queen*. I'll tell him about Patrick Henry *and* about Oliver Cromwell. Elvis Presley *and* the Beatles. Because having a sense of place is part of your emotional inheritance. Like sunshine, it adds to the sweetness of life.

April 4, 1996

MORNING HAS BROKEN

THIS is a mother who does not like Mother's Day. Although I am told that Mothering Sunday is as old and English as apple crumble, Mother's Day, with its greeting cards and bright flowers, feels as American to me as hypochondria, litigation and the mall.

But this Mother's Day was different. It began on the Friday at Sam's primary school which had a special assembly in our honour. As we sat in the gym on the baby-bear size chairs waiting for our children to file in, I thought about what we mothers have in common on this day, two days after Dunblane. From the time we heard the first news reports, we have been unsettled to the very roots of our beings. Because, as mothers, our main aim in life is to create a world in which our children are central and safe.

In Sam's school, the children are the beneficiaries of decaffeinated, nicotine-free and mainly alcohol-free pregnancies. Scanned before birth and baby monitored after, they have been breast-fed and placed on their backs for safe sleeping. When old enough to be entrusted to the care of their teachers, they were strapped in consumer-tested car seats and delivered to their carefully chosen country school. Protecting them – physically and emotionally – is the single most important thing we do in our lives.

The eight-year-olds enter first, then the six and seven-year-olds. Sam searches the rows of motherly faces, and when he sees me he shyly smiles. When the five-year-olds come in, we all study them with care. Five-year-olds suddenly look terribly vulnerable. As they begin to sing *Morning has Broken*, I say a silent, guilty prayer of thanks that I am a thousand miles from Dunblane. That I am still a mother today.

This Mother's Day to be a mother is to be in limbo. In an ideal world we would like to abide by the rules of a village civilisation, the injunctions of pastoral people. We are not the first generation of mothers who cannot protect our children from the horrors of the outside world, but we are the first to be bringing up our children in a world in which insanely powerful guns are so easily available.

I know we cannot build a barricade that will protect our children from the violence about us, but I will join the campaign to make all hand guns illegal. I know all the arguments against the ban. The one that irritates most defends hand guns because they are used in Olympic sports. Big deal. I have watched as these guns have changed the very heart and soul of American life. In this country there is still – just – time to stop the madness. Take my word. We defend the rights of the lovers of semi-automatic pistols at our peril.

* * *

SIGNS of spring have been highly intermittent in our corner of Suffolk. We would not know it was spring at Wyken except that the peacocks and cockerels are obsessed with desire. The objects of their desire, hens and peahens alike, look as if they have permanent headaches.

Apparently, serious gardeners prefer seeing gardens at this time of year. They talk about their structure. Our gardens are open now but I am too embarrassed to charge until the daffodils can provide a little interest. All we have showing is what I call dirt and my husband calls soil. We have just put out the garden seats and rocking chairs, newly repainted in various shades of blue, grey-blue and blue-green. I inherited my grandmother's dislike of white garden furniture, a feeling she shared with Nancy Lancaster who said 'it looks like aspirin in the garden'.

Unfortunately the peacocks now prefer the seats to the trees, and as seats and peacocks are my principal contribution to the gardens it is my job to clean the mess. During his presidency I rarely felt sympathy for George Bush, but now, when I start the day with a bucket of hot, soapy water, I smile as I remember him saying he was 'in deep doodoo'. I know just how he felt.

March 28, 1996

THE LAST LADY

IN 1961 our history teacher assigned us a scrapbook project to do during the year. We could choose anyone, dead or alive, who had a relationship with history. Nearly every girl in the class chose Jackie Kennedy. I chose Abraham Lincoln. I bore the burden of my mistake for nine months, a time when the whole world was wallpapered with the pages from *LIFE* magazine: Jackie the teenager on a horse, Jackie the bride marrying the senator, Jackie the mother swinging baby Caroline in the air, Jackie the First Lady at the inaugural balls, Jackie (always pronounced Zhak-leen, not Jack-a-lynn) showing a *savoir-faire* to Charles de Gaulle. My best friend's scrapbook was in the shape of a size ten shoe, Jackie's shoe size. All I had were three black and white postcards and a copy of the Gettysburg Address.

To compensate for my error I have, 35 years later, forked out £41 for the Sotheby's catalogue of the April 23-25 estate sale of Jaqueline Kennedy Onassis. It is the mother of all scrapbooks.

Jackie Kennedy was as close as America ever got to having an aristocracy, a classy lady in a so-called classless society. She had a valuable gift, what my grandmother called 'an intelligent silence'. During her lifetime her silence grew beside her like a tree. Although she graciously gave the nation a tour of the White House, no citizens of *The World of Interiors* ever got a peak at her Manhattan dining room.

No interviews, no confessions, no revelations. Until she died, America never even knew she smoked a pack a day. We eventually learned that her childhood was grim, that her marriage to the president was no day on the beach and that her brief marriage to Onassis was no Skorpios. Experienced in tragedy, Jackie had a will and inner discipline more regal than anything Bagehot could have dreamt of. She led the most private of public lives and the most public of private lives, but her lips were sealed. That is how she maintained her magic and her popularity. There is a lesson to be learned here.

So why are her children selling all their mama's stuff? Their mama, who thought privacy was next to godliness? How can they sell their father's famous rocking chair (lot 1194, estimate $3,000-5,000); the rocking horse in Caroline's nursery in the White House (lot 32, estimate $2,000-3,000); Aaron Shikler's portraits of her children (lots 1178-1185)? By all means sell that diamond the size of a cockroach that Onassis (5ft 5in) gave Jackie (5ft 7in) on their engagement (lot 452, estimate $500,000), but why part with her gold charm bracelet (lot 363, estimate $1,500-2,000)?

The problem is this: Jackie's children are city folks. Country people hang onto things. They have a sense of the past and they have room. When the attics are full, stuff is carried to the outbuildings. In the country, each generation adds its layer to life. Jackie was a countrywoman. Although she spoke French and spent most of her adult life in cities, she grew up in Virginia hunt country, a world more English country house than *Brideshead Revisited*. Photographs of Jackie's Manhattan flat (seen for the first time in the Sotheby's catalogue) show a dower house set in Central Park: slightly shabby, bookish, civilised, calm.

But there is another reason behind splitting up their mother's treasured possessions. Caroline and John grew up as rich kids in the world's richest land. Their mother grew up surrounded by wealth but with no financial security. Throughout her life she held onto her stuff like a farmer holds onto his land. Her main crops were style, beauty and silence. Although the sale will take four days and includes 1,195 lots, I like to think that her real legacy is rather more.

April 11, 1996

PROPERTY RIGHTS

LIKE HRH the Princess of Wales, I study with some diligence the property pages of COUNTRY LIFE. I think I could pass an exam on the most magnificent estates on offer during the past 12 months. When the photographs and descriptions are truly breathtaking ('One of Scotland's foremost sporting estates with an historic castle in a spectacular setting'), I get the particulars. As my purchasing power is nil, this may seem a triste activity. It certainly embarrasses my husband who is unaware that I order these in his name.

I hanker after moats, Gothic and Scottish, but my real passion is for provenance. I wish COUNTRY LIFE ran 'Who Lives Here Now' features on the houses that have appeared in its pages over the years. I want to know the owners, the prices paid, the renovations to house and garden, and, most of all, reasons for sale. This probably smacks of an architectural *Hello!* My curiosity intensifies as I reflect glumly that the only British people able to purchase some of these properties are lottery winners and a princess.

So does it really matter who purchases the magnificent castle and sporting estate in Caithness, in all about 30,000 acres (COUNTRY LIFE, March 7, offers over £3 million)? If I were the property police, who would I choose as future proprietors of the Dunbeath Estate (and Dunbeath Castle dating from the 15th century, recently renovated to a high standard, according to the particulars): the two-earringed, felonious lottery winner or the German shooting syndicate? Does it matter if a little 400-acre corner of Berkshire is forever the £100 million holiday skeikhdom of Sheikh Zayed Bin Sultan Al Nayyan and his 12 wives and 30 children?

Tim Finney once asked me such questions on Radio 4's *Farming Today*. We were standing in the vineyard and looking onto Bill Morley's farm, 400 acres that march alongside our land. It had just been bought by a German industrialist. I admit we wanted the land. We spent weeks walking the fields and meeting agricultural accountants at Binder Hamlyn. In the end we lacked courage. Although I was brought up in the religion of the Mississippi Delta – always buy the land adjoining your own because you may get only one chance – I was also brought up surrounded by the 'land poor' which means lots of acres and not a dime in the bank. But my reply was an edgy: 'Yes, it does matter who owns the land.' Bill Morley is an outstanding farmer. He nurtures his fields and his crops show it. He genuinely cares about his farmworkers. Above all, he is not an absentee landlord.

My objections are not down to snobbery, which I frankly deplore. It is what another Southerner who made England her home, Nancy Lancaster, called 'appropriateness'. She used the word about decorating houses. She believed that a cottage ought not be decorated like Versailles, that Laura Ashley florals are not appropriate for Versailles.

I think it's appropriate when farmers who know and love the land farm it; when big country houses are occupied, Mitfordstyle, by a succession of 'bucolic squires, their wives, their enormous families, their dogs, their horses, their father's relict, and their unmarried sisters'. Of course, the wives can be foreign. American heiresses have been useful in the past and a mournful lament in my own marriage is: 'your family's been in America 200 years and they don't even have a chain of gas stations?'

But above all, I think it is appropriate for the people who own large hunks of land to live on it and to play a part in the life of the community. I'm not sure whether this makes me a Bolshevik or a target of the Bolsheviks. I've been both. I'd like to think I've mellowed over the years and now I'm just an appropriatist.

April 18, 1996

LEAVING LLOYD'S

MY Mississippi grandmother believed that all life revolved round love and money: 'The rest is just conversation'. That was Jane Austen's opinion, too. All of her finest first paragraphs, indeed her first lines, include money. Like the opening blast of *Emma*: 'Emma Woodhouse, handsome, clever and rich.' I love the frankness about how much everyone is worth and, more important, their annual income.

In *Pride and Prejudice*, Mr Darcy tops the money chart with his income of £10,000 a year. His friend Bingley has inherited 'nearly an hundred thousand pounds' which produces an income of £4,000 to £5,000. Each of the Bingley sisters has a fortune of £20,000 – or five times the sum that Mrs Bennet brought to her marriage. Mr Bennet's income is £2,000 a year, a fifth of Darcy's, less than half of Bingley's and, considerably more than Miss Austen's family, who managed on just £600 a year.

Then there is land ownership. Elizabeth ponders 'how

many people's happiness were in his guardianship' as she tours Pemberley. Mr Bingley's money comes from the North – industry and commerce – and his sisters long for him to purchase an estate because only land ownership, that verdant sign of old money, can put them into the more agreeable shade of aristocracy.

But economically alert as she was, Miss Austen never created a character who was a Name at Lloyd's of London. She well might have. I know from the Wedgwood ashtray sent to us in 1988 on their tercentenary that Lloyd's was over a century old when Miss Austen was writing her novels. How I wish she had written about, say, a widow whose husband dies in the Napoleonic Wars, leaving her a house but no income. A dashing young underwriter persuades her to become a member of Lloyd's and, before you can say sense and stupidity, all is lost.

When I first read Jane Austen, I had a picture of the English as a people candid and clear about the importance of money. Now I understand that financial openness is largely a feminine English quality.

I know five farmers within a ten-mile radius of us who have now received their 'finality', the supposedly final lifeboat from Lloyd's that will help Names get their affairs in order. Not one of them – we had dinner with two last week – would dream of discussing it. My husband is one of those Englishmen who never discuss money and think it is unacceptable to grumble. Lloyd's most remarkable achievement is to convince so many Names that it is they who are personally either stupid or greedy. Names still don't seem to understand that some of the people they were dealing with were crooks who, were they living in America, would now be in jail. I am from the old school – let's just call it the Jane Austen school – where money is serious business. Southern manners spare him my buckin' and snortin' at a dinner party, but here in the more Austenian pages of COUNTRY LIFE I can defend all those tongue-tied English farmers hit by the shenanigans at Lloyd's.

I don't believe that accepting this latest offer is good for the Names or good for the future of Lloyd's. If they really want a happy ending, Lloyd's must follow Miss Austen's example and provide a true finality in which a line is ineradicably drawn with the past. It's the Names who occupy the moral high ground.

Meanwhile, I dream of the day when I can say 'halleluja, free at last'. When I can wake up to Radio 4's *Today* programme and listen to reports of hurricanes, oil spills, plane crashes, bombs and fatal diseases, and feel the joy of pure heartbreak, untainted by grim and guilty thoughts such as 'Oh Lord, does this affect Lloyd's?' I want what Jane Austen would have called 'difficult, ordinary unhappiness'.

April 25, 1996

THE DOOMED DUCHESS

I GOT married two days after HRH the Duchess of York. When I arrived at the Crypt Chapel of the Palace of Westminster there were long queues of people across the road waiting to see the royal wedding flowers in Westminster Abbey. My nephew, aged seven, thought the crowds were waiting to see me. I was about to give a big wave with my bouquet when he whispered 'Aunt Carla, you look just like a mermaid.'

But this July I will be celebrating my tenth wedding anniversary and the Duchess will be divorced. Ever since I heard the news I have been mulling over why I've been a survivor in the marriage stakes and the Duchess has not. Believe me, I don't feel smug. I just feel terrifyingly lucky.

I would put it this way: all marriages begin the same, booby-trapped with our wild expectations and hopes, our individual flaws which we have polished since childhood, and the awful understanding of our modern age, that if we have to call the whole thing off, it won't be a disaster.

Maybe I started my married life with a few advantages over Sarah Ferguson. I have grateful memories of a country childhood, a home full of books, a grandmother who took up the slack left by parents who were eager to get back to lives that had been suspended by the war. These are the things that will give you judgment, and judgment is one thing that both the Duke and Duchess appear to have lacked.

From the day she said 'I will,' the Duchess has been in trouble for her bad taste: bad taste in clothes, bad taste in home decoration, bad taste in financial advisers and finance. The Duke has been condemned solely for his bad taste in wife. But taste is only the most visible dimension of judgment.

To be fair, the Duke and Duchess never got to experience the sheltered simplicity that two people newly married need and deserve. Time to lay down the foundation that leads to a deeper relationship which in turn brings duration and continuity to marriage. Maybe time wouldn't have helped. Perhaps they were too selfish or too cynical from the start. But I still believe that simple, unencumbered time together helps more than anything.

An old friend once told me that 'marriage is like driving a car at night. You can see only as far as your headlights but you can make the whole trip that way.' No one knows what the journey will look like; you just have to stay on the road.

I wish somebody had passed that advice on to the Duchess. She needed a wise and chic godmother to keep her on the road. Someone witty and warm in neutral colours, able to give advice about glamourous men and free airfares (just say no); who understood the red-headed Duchess's spirit and intelligence and enthusiasm and knew how to use it.

And maybe this wise woman could have persuaded the Duchess before it was too late, that open marriage, however enlightened the concept might feel, doesn't work. Somebody gets hurt, and then somebody gets out. Alas, for her and us, there was no such godmother. Now the Duchess is truly on her own. I think it would behove all those leader writers who have been writing 'good riddance' now to back off.

I for one wish this woman some peace. Her happiness and serenity is the greatest gift she can now give to her girls. When the Duke and Duchess are together they touch and protect each other. I think that means a lot to their daughters. It probably means something to all those people who waited that hot afternoon ten years ago to see the flowers that decorated the beginning of another doomed marriage.

May 2, 1996

STEALING PLEASURE

'A giver gets no pleasure in a letter acknowledging kindness three weeks late even though it crawls with apologies – you will have stolen pleasure from one who has tried to give it to you.'

THAT message was taped to the package my grandmother sent to me my first week at college. Inside was a Sheaffer fountain pen, a box of Crane writing paper and a volume of the letters of Scott Fitzgerald, my literary idol at the time. The quote was from a letter he wrote in 1940 to his daughter, Scottie, during her first year at Vassar.

But whereas I love fountain pens, blue-black ink and creamy writing paper, not a day passes when I am not stealing pleasure from someone who has tried to give it to me. What is this neurotic inability to write anything like a prompt letter of gratitude? Why does the moon have to be in full eclipse before I can write a long, introspective letter, the kind that holds friendships together?

In the urban world, telephones and postcards disguise the socially derelict. But in the country, the ritual of correspondence is central and real.

Country people are the last real letter-writers. There may be a fax machine in the farm office, but personal letters are written with Parker pens that belonged to a grandfather, on writing paper that still has three-digit telephone numbers and no post codes. Letters are written at writing desks. Beds may be shared but desks, never: she has hers, he has his. Envelopes and stamps are always in their place, and those exquisite little scales used in drug movies for weighing cocaine are used in the country for weighing letters.

I inherited my mother-in-law's writing desk. Which is not to say that it is actually mine, but that as long as I am mistress of this house I can – if only I could – write my letters at this desk. Although Ralph Lauren would kill for this walnut desk with its labradors in silver frames, French pewter lamp and bowl of camellias, here I have never written a word.

For a start, I have never been able to bring myself to acquire those note cards with my married name and address printed above a line. In the same vein, I am almost always at home but I could never be At Home. But the real problem lies deeper: the greater my indebtedness, the greater my paralysis. If you loan me your Hoover, I can write three pages of poetry. Provide me with shelter and comfort for three days, and I am incapacitated with gratitude. I will suffer sleepless nights for months rather than sit down and write 'I so enjoyed...'

I've watched ancient friendships collapse when godchildren did not respond swiftly and gratefully to godparents, so I'm doing my best to instil in my child a sense of duty and gratitude. Last year these sessions ended in hysterics (mine) and tears (his). In January I listened to a harrowing account on the radio about a little girl with a brain tumour. The mother described how her daughter, then undiagnosed, had cried in pain all of Christmas but 'I made her write all her thank-you notes.' I know this Everywoman.

One day psychologists will probably show that faithful letter-writers are more socially competent and personally effective, more self-reliant and trustworthy, less likely to go to pieces or freeze under stress. My only consolation is that I have decided to write a book called *Letters I Wish I Had Written.*

This will be no slim volume. In it I will finally give thanks to people who gave me dinners with rare and irreplaceable bottles of wine, and thanks to the long-lost friends who gave me insight and hope. When every letter is written, the relief will feel like heaven.

Yours very truly.

May 9, 1996

MORAL HEYDAY

THE great loves of my life have been dogs, wine and literature. As I grew up in the last state to repeal the law of Prohibition, wine was not easily available. My first sips came at my Confirmation, with the port-like wine used in our high-church Episcopal mass. I loved it.

Literature was easier to come by. I nearly blinded myself reading *Tom Sawyer* in the hot Delta sun and spent the next three weeks confined to a darkened room. For years I tried to convert the kudzu-covered hills of Mississippi into the wild Yorkshire moors of the Brontës, where I was more at home than in the highly cultivated gardens of Jane Austen.

But my everlasting literary heroine is Dorothea Brooke in *Middlemarch*. Unlike her I could never willingly deprive myself of pleasure, but I passionately share her ardour to do good. One of my favourite scenes in literature is Dorothea bent over her designs for estate cottages. She understood that true charity must begin at home; only then can any real social good be accomplished.

With my marriage I believed, like Dorothea, that my moral heyday had come. On our land adjoining the village I would build low-cost housing for villagers who had been edged out of the housing market. What I really wanted to do was create a whole and perfect village like the one James Gladstone had designed for Upper Donnington (defeated by small-minded planners in 1988). My beloved husband, no Casaubon he, reluctantly told me we would go bankrupt. Our alternative was to sell a couple of acres of land at the agricultural rate, where shared equity homes could be built for a housing association. The only hitch to our generosity: I would retain a say in the design and planning. As George Eliot so wisely understood, reforming passion is streaked with egoism.

The architect's first plans contained everything you hate: anonymous brick ('low maintenance'), reddish-brown-stained windows, ('low maintenance'), two styles of stick-on porch ('individualising'). But nothing prepared me for the dimensions inside. No space for a hat rack or a pushchair in the entrance. A kitchen that would fit inside a camper van. A bathroom with one of those baths you find in cheap French hotels. Not a single built-in cupboard and no space for wardrobes. The second bedroom could fit only one single bed but no table and bedside light beside it.

Surely, I wailed, there are building codes requiring new dwellings to have minimum dimensions before something can be called a bedroom, a bathroom? But no, the government has done away with these, the Parker Morris standards, thus freeing the house builders to create rooms of inhumane dimensions ('market forces').

I offered more land (free) if they would enlarge the living space. I refused to budge unless the exteriors were plastered and painted in various Suffolk colourwashes, with painted windows and doors. I demanded full-length porches. As I left each meeting I could hear audible groans through the door.

I was no more loved in the village than by the developers. Residents of the houses adjoining the site no longer chatted in the village shop. Leyland hedges went up like a rural iron curtain.

Like Dorothea, I found the world around me was beginning to cramp my ardour. Still, this is not a study in defeated aspiration: the houses got built, and their colours of yellow and terracotta and pale green provide warmth and welcome to the village. The people who live in them like them.

When the grand opening arrived, my husband was invited to preside over the ceremony. I was asked to provide the tea. How seamlessly art is bound to life. In the final line of that great work George Eliot writes of the good done by those 'who lived faithfully a hidden life'. Although in truth, for this I could do with more practice.

May 16, 1996

HEAD GARDENER

BEFORE I really went anywhere I gave up travelling. My reputation back home is that of vagabond, not adventurer. Even my dramatic departure from the land of my birth was not my idea but a journey sponsored by the Ku Klux Klan which took an immoderate dislike to my politics and manners. I should probably be grateful for those burning crosses that lit my exit, because in my heart I know I am as sedentary as a tree.

Here in the countryside this reluctance to go anywhere is a blessing. All round me are people who have never been to Newmarket (25 miles away), much less to London (100 miles). Perhaps this contentment to live the rest of my life in a country the size of Oregon is premature, but I relish the freedom from the yearning to be somewhere else.

On Saturday we had a gala lunch party in honour of our gardener, John Mann. In our transient age, John is the saint of permanence. He came to this village in Suffolk as a child during the Second World War and at the age of 15 began work here in the garden at Wyken. He has spent every working day here for the past 50 years.

When he began as a 'garden boy', my husband's great-aunt was living here on her own. Her only son had bought Wyken in 1920. In 1931 he became Member of Parliament for Bury St Edmunds, Conservative and unopposed. He died in a train crash on his way to the House of Commons in 1944. Two years later, John found himself on an estate still in mourning for its master.

In 1946 Wyken included 30 farm workers, two gardeners, a chauffeur, a gamekeeper, a housekeeper, a cook, a bevy of maids, 12 Suffolk Punches, a herd of pedigree Friesians, 180 acres of ancient woodland, 850 acres under the plough, and a cricket pitch in the front meadow. The garden gave more acreage to Brussels sprouts and gooseberries than herbaceous borders. The first job assigned to John was the renovation of lawns that had been left to grow during the war when petrol was too scarce to be used for mowing.

During his half-century at Wyken, John has seen a revolution in the countryside. The farm – with the same acreage under the plough – is now farmed by two men. The Friesians were sold in the 1960s in favour of arable farming. When my husband came here to farm in the Seventies he discovered that his real love was botany, a passion which soon spilled over into gardening.

He became 'garden boy' to John's head gardener, and the two of them converted an old orchard into a rose garden. Borders became knot-gardens; shrubberies turned into herb gardens; a field became a maze. My only contributions have been the pursuit of timelessness: five rocking chairs on a make-believe verandah that gets the setting sun; a graveyard where noble dogs and humans can rest side by side in eternal peace.

As the burdens on John have grown with each wild and expansive dream, he has never said a discouraging word. He baulks only at attention to himself. As is the way with saints, he is modest beyond measure. Few people have witnessed so closely the changes in the countryside as this boyish, gentle, patient man and fewer still have lived lives of such natural continuity.

I have lived in three countries but I feel that the immigrant and the gardener have this in common: long tap roots which seek nourishment deep beneath the surface of the earth. To transplant us is a perilous job requiring great tenderness. Snap the root and the plant dies. I hope I'm here to stay. John, who retired on Saturday, returns to work on Monday to begin his new (part-time) job as propagator-in-chief.

May 30, 1996

SWAN SONG

I WAS born on the banks of the Yazoo River. Yazoo is the Choctaw Indian word for death. It's always felt like pay day in my southern Gothic soul just knowing that I was born on the River of Death.

When I was small my grandparents and I would get into their green Packard on Sunday afternoons and drive out to look at the crops. These were cotton and soy beans. Cotton is a beautiful plant, with red blossoms that turn white, and veiny, green leaves. Soy beans never interested me. Nothing I knew was made of soy beans and nobody ate them. This was a 'government crop' – a subsidy crop. After we had walked miles down the rows, hunting for boll weevils, we would get back in the car to go down to the river and look at the swans.

Nothing could have looked more out of place in the hot, dusty landscape of the Delta than these regal, ivory birds gliding on the mud-brown river, as exoctic as colonial English women at a garden party in a remote hill station in India.

The swans were all that was left of a money-making scheme started by a man from Memphis called Ray Moon and his son Little Ray. He had come down here with an incubator full of swans' eggs. Painted on the side of his Chevrolet pick-up was Son and Moon Bird Farm. He sold swan eggs for $2 each to everybody in the Delta who had some water on their land. He promised to come back in a year's time to buy the birds back for $25 each. The returns looked even better than for soy beans.

We never knew what happened to Son and Moon but the swans hatched out and encountered the elements that made life hard for all of us: foxes, racoons, snakes. Some died from what my Aunt Blanche calls the 'heat prostitution'. Those swans that managed to survive the first summer soon left the confines of pond life and took to the river. There they became tough and crazy in the way soldiers do who go native. Even the alligators left them alone. But on Sunday afternoons families would sit in their cars, drink Cokes and watch the swans glide past like southern belles in the backseats of convertibles in the homecoming parade.

I hadn't thought about these swans for 30 years until we visited a fruit farm in Essex. Its owners have recently diversified. In a large alleyway between the apple trees, they have a compound with eight ostriches. They thought we might be interested in a pair. Somehow, if you have diversified into anything (and we have seven acres of vines, a vineyard restaurant and country store) people think you are just biding your time before branching out into llamas, old train engines, home-grown truffles and boar hunts.

I have to admit the ostriches are impressive. They are enormous, although they look badly designed. They are also expensive: a mature bird can cost £15,000. There are now reckoned to be 350 ostrich farms in Britain with as many as 10,000 birds. The smoothest-talking entrepreneurs are behind the Ostrich Farming Corporation based in Belgium. They've been selling folks ostriches which the buyers will never lay eyes on.

It sounds pretty good: lower in fat than turkey, higher in protein than beef, no BSE, acceptable to all religious faiths, great shoes and handbags. Ostrich meat costs more at Harrods than *foie gras de canard frais*.

But I'm getting older and wiser. For instance, I know that to make wine you have to sell wine. As Yeats put it: 'In dreams begin responsibilities.' And somehow I can't get Ray and Little Ray and the Yazoo swans out of my mind.

June 6, 1996

MILDEW ON THE MAGNOLIAS

MY friend Katie lives on a chicken farm in Wales. She tends her chickens by day and writes thrillers at night. After working for several years on a story in which all the victims die of salmonella poisoning, she decided that to publish might be bad for business. This year she started a new book. The action takes place at the Chelsea Flower Show.

I'd like to tell you the plot but it might be bad for business. My husband has just joined the council of the Royal Horticultural Society and I don't think he would like it if I wrote about killer carnivorous plants and murder among the medals. He draws the line at mildew on the magnolias.

All the same, Katie's manuscript contains useful advice for anyone wanting to get the most out of the world's grandest flower show. For instance, enter by the Chelsea Embankment and you are immersed in the magical world of the cameo gardens. Choose the Royal Hospital Road entrance, and your morale is filled with a sense of misadventure: the St John Ambulance tent, the acre of public loos, wheelchairs lined up like supermarket trolleys.

Go early to avoid the crowds. I was dubious about that, but Katie produced official attendance charts. Between eight and ten in the morning you virtually have the place to yourself and 10,000 other people. From noon onwards, you are surrounded by 40,000 garden lovers, all of whom know their acid from their lime.

And don't wear a hat unless it is a rain hat with a brim or sun-hat that you would wear in your own garden. You will feel silly. Even HM the Queen dispensed with her hat this year in favour of one of those veils that look like a hairnet.

When I told Katie that I would be at Chelsea on the Monday (a marital perk) she said: 'Good. I need a fact-checker.' To those unfamiliar with this term, a fact-checker is usually an aspiring writer whose first job is poring over the manuscripts of other writers in search of exaggeration, inaccuracy, lazy truth.

Katie's got the fact-checker's pertinacity. Are the duchess's eyes really iris blue? (Yes, *Iris reticulata* Cantab, if I got the right duchess.) Is the marquee still the largest in the world? Yes, all three-and-a-half acres of it.

I explain that I am not in the Royal entourage and therefore unable to verify the Queen's knowledge of *Helleborus dumetorum*. 'Of course you can,' snaps Katie, who could eat her dear chicken named Fanny roasted with garlic and never shed a tear. The only Royal hearsay I procure is this: Queen, gazing at front cottage garden (Webbs of Wychbold on Sun Flower Street:) 'Look, a cannon. And crenellated box.' Garden designer: 'Yes, Ma'am. The theme is 'An Englishman's Home is His Castle.' Hearty laugh from Queen. I was charmed by this tentative exchange. 'Useless,' responds Katie to this bit of insider dealing.

I let her down again at the gala evening, a corporate entertainment exercise that feels like Glyndebourne without Mozart. I couldn't remember the exact price of the tickets. I verified that the champagne is free, a fact that may have affected my yearning for truth.

The problem is that I'm more Barbara Pym than P. D. James. I prefer subtlety to the hard edge of fact. My most cherished souvenir of the show was a Scottish woman explaining 'this bulbocodium is shy to flower unless really happy'. But I think setting a thriller in the Chelsea Flower Show is inspired. A world as self-contained as Agatha Christie's boats and trains, its elements are beauty, nature, talent, commerce and ambition. The atmosphere is filled with audacious metaphors and illusions. I'm thinking of buying the film rights.

June 13, 1996

SUFFOLK SHOW

WHAT you call cow parsley, I grew up calling Queen Anne's lace. I'm glad we got the fancier name. Just saying Queen Anne's lace made me feel rich, like having a new dress even if it had been my sister's first.

I love it when the country lanes shrink in width, their edges disappearing under the lush green growth. The mists of cow parsley almost hide the new roadsigns, an epidemic that has spread mercilessly in the past year. These aggressive metal blasts warn us of ancient and familiar bridges and friendly narrow lanes. They pollute our country roads and deprive us of the one true privilege of country life, the feeling of timelessness. They make me think of desperate little countries whose economic decline is accompanied by ever more grandiose postage stamps.

Last week we sheared the sheep, an ancient ceremony transformed by electric shears into an afternoon's work. I watch my bewildered ewes as the shearer wrestles them onto their haunches and strips them of their coats. I

36

see shame in their sheepish faces. Shorn and forlorn, they look like goats.

The sheep we take to the Suffolk Show are spared this humiliation. Their indignity is confined to halter training. John, our farm manager, has been working with seven-year-old Sam for weeks in preparation for the young handlers' class.

We park in the vice-president's car park, our non-air-conditioned Volvo outclassed by the herd of new Land Rovers, Audi A4s and BMWs. This is arable country and the truth is, we've never had it so good. I'm a farmer born and bred, so all I think about is when the boom will end. But consider this: prices for farmland in Norfolk – as good a guide as any – are £4,000 an acre, the highest since the Second World War.

At the show, the talk is of rain. We've had only one inch since March 1st. We usually average six inches in spring. The crops on the light land have used up the reserves and are now suffering from what farmers somewhat prosaically call a 'moisture deficit'.

In the East Anglian wine tent our stand looks like school prize day with our 1995 English Wine of the Year, East Anglian Wine of the Year and Wine Guild trophies. I say when you've got it, flaunt it. Last year's frost on May 8th was a killer. It takes only half an hour at $31°F$ to kill new growth in a vine. We lost 80% of the crop. Instead of making 20,000 bottles last year, we made 3,000.

In the National Farmers Union tent I recognise the farmer who is putting up sheds on the edge of our village for 150,000 chickens. I avoid his gaze. One of the most depressing side-effects of the beef scare is that now everybody is eating chicken like crazy and feeling virtuous. Well, chicken-eaters, I don't want to rain on your parade but the broiler bird in your supermarket is only 45 days old when it is killed. In its month-and-a-half of life, the chicken will put on 5lb. This is no miracle: it is the result of packing the birds together so that they can't move, lacing their food with growth stimulants and drugging them with antibiotics. It's salmonella city.

By the time we get to the young handlers' event I wish I had brought my vial of Rescue Remedy, the homeopathic answer to Prozac that no farmer should be without. But when I see Sam with his Shetland ewe Lulu, I cheer up. Lulu is an orphaned lap-sheep who spent her babyhood in our house. Sam is practising dominance and Lulu is so loyal that she co-operates. Out of a class of 21, Sam comes second. When he is presented with his blue ribbon there is a crescendo of applause. For one brief, shining moment, country life feels as perfect as the final scene in *Babe*.

June 20, 1996

ICKWORTH REVISITED

Fade in on a licence plate starkly visible in the blizzard. It reads 888 NOB.

Pull back to reveal a 1964 Rolls Royce Silver Cloud, stuck in a snowdrift.

Interior: red leather seats. Behind the steering wheel is an elegantly dressed man in his early forties. He clutches his mobile telephone to his swollen, once handsome, aristocratic face. A Land Rover Discovery arrives. A cheerful balding man in a smart Barbour gets out. He studies the beached green car.

Credits start to roll.

What we see: Rolls Royce being towed by Land Rover Discovery through the vast park of a great English country house.

Title: *Ickworth Revisited.*

This is as far as I've got on my new screenplay but I'm told the opening scene is critical. Few directors read past the second page, and it's all there: life or death situation, dramatic rescue, humour and grandeur.

You may think this reads suspiciously like *Brideshead Revisited,* but in Hollywood they say there are only three stories in the world but a million ways to tell them. Mr Waugh set his narrative between the wars, in a framework of prologue and epilogue. Charles Ryder, billeted in the great country house he once knew so well, tells the story. For *Ickworth Revisited,* a true story set 50 years later, the narrator is James Miller, the Sotheby's director who answers the distress call made by Frederick William John Augustus Hervey, Seventh Marquess of Bristol, aka John Bristol. John may not be as whimsical as Sebastian Flyte but he has a talent for flight. Miller is a modern-day Ryder: 18th-century works of art expert and blessed with a Land Rover.

Inside the country house the Marquess assures his carnivorous wolfhounds that the stranger is a friend. Meanwhile Miller gazes appreciatively at the contents, recalling 20 years earlier when the Sixth Marquess removed it all and put it up for auction.

FLASHBACK to five-year-old John running up the drive to meet his papa who has had a long and unsuccessful day in the courts trying to prove his son is illegitimate. Truth is, Victor Bristol is one of the world's meanest daddies. By the next scene little John is a fatherless child. Like Lord Marchmain who becomes an exile in Venice with his mistress, Lord Bristol decamps to the south of France with his mistress, leaving a bare east wing at Ickworth.

The now 20-year-old John Bristol uses all his energy, cunning and talent to buy back his rightful treasures, an heroic endeavour which costs him £2.6 million back in 1975. He succeeds in reassembling his legacy. After all, this has been the seat of his family for 500 years. But whereas Sebastian Flyte becomes a soppy alcoholic, in this tale of English aristocracy in the 1990s, John Bristol gets hooked on drugs. Instead of becoming a saintly down-and-out like Sebastian, John spends two spells in prison for possession of heroin and cocaine.

Life on the outside isn't easy for the Marquess, however. The English winters and the National Trust are getting to him. Once again, Miller comes to his rescue: Sotheby's will sell the contents. Just as Sebastian Flyte finds peace in North Africa, John Bristol can find happiness in the Bahamas.

Inside the marquee we see the Rolls Royce (lot 610, estimate £30,000). In the east wing we see the paintings, carpets, pictures, all with labels and lot numbers. On the billiard table are bound copies of COUNTRY LIFE, 1901-1906 (lot 406, estimate £400), family albums and visitors books. For some of the guests at the private view this is too much. But the message is as pure as the opening shots of snow: there must be more to life than having everything.

July 27 1996

THE SECOND SEX

SOMEWHERE along life's highway I lost my 'Sisterhood is Powerful' T-shirt. I still have my copy of Simone de Beauvoir's *The Second Sex*, although I never actually finished it. It's a souvenir of the past, recalling those heady days when I felt thrillingly superior to every woman in a Volvo estate full of children and labradors.

Somehow country life isn't fertile territory for radical feminism. Maybe it's the way female animals – ewes, hens, doe-eyed cows – are so relaxed in their superiority to the males. Maybe it's the whole domestic set-up.

All the same, last week I felt a small surge of what we used to call sisterly solidarity. It started with the COUNTRY LIFE interview with the Marchioness of Worcester (June 6). In case you missed this, Ms Ward, aka Tracy Worcester, aka Lady Worcester, is a very beautiful woman, wife of the future Duke of Beaufort and mama of a future, future Duke. I reckon if she'd just stuck with tiaras and babies, everyone would think she was adorable.

But Ms Ward is also a passionate defender of the environment and this drives people crazy. Ms Ward is worried about many things, such as the greenhouse effect (a world dying of thirst); the hole in the ozone layer (skin cancer); air pollution (childhood asthma). Although I have never met Ms Ward, I share every one of her concerns.

So when we went to lunch at a gathering of East Anglia's more prosperous farming community, I was interested to hear the conversation get round to the COUNTRY LIFE interview. 'Ghastly woman,' grumped 1,100 acres in the Brecklands. 'Can't stand her,' gruffed 6,000 acres from Norfolk. Then a warm thump on my back sent my wine flying: 'She lacks your common sense, my dear.' Suddenly I felt I was drinking with the enemy.

The truth is, women and men view the environment differently. Ask a man if he'd steal a loaf to feed his starving family and he answers no, citing rules of justice. Women, rather more involved in the food chain, always say yes, citing human compassion. Women make moral judgments based on emotional ideas such as caring. Men are guided by abstract notions.

Which brings me to the thorny issue at the end of the interview. So how is it, asked the interviewer, that she is on the council of the Soil Association but the tens of thousands of acres under her husband's care are not farmed organically?

Snap. I'm not a board member and our farm barely

stretches to 1,000 acres. Sensitive we may be but organic, I regret to say, we are not. Men (even those who marry smart girls) are attached to the status quo. They run MAFF and the NFU. They dream up and sustain the CAP. They love words like efficient, competitive, productive.

Women feed children. They worry about nitrates, pesticide residues and antibiotics in animal feed. I'm not saying that women are the patron saints of the earth. We're the ones who have demanded picture-perfect vegetables and cheap meat; we push the trolleys that carry the Spanish strawberries and French cherries while hundreds of acres of fruit trees in the Fens are destroyed. We depend on fast food for our temporary sanity.

But I think if farmers (by and large a manly lot) are to be convinced that it is important and profitable to produce quality food responsibly and humanely, it will only come from fussy, pushy women.

This time round I'd like to think we in the sisterhood might concentrate less on our psyches and more on the earth. Meanwhile I'm considering going to the T-shirt shop in Cambridge and designing one that says 'Right on, Trace.'

July 4, 1996

IN TOUCH WITH ELEANOR

I'VE always thought that if Hillary Clinton had had a country childhood, she never would have married Bill. There is something about growing up surrounded by cows and chickens and car batteries mounted onto tree stumps that leaves you immune to pick-up lines about watermelon. Which isn't to say she wouldn't have voted for him – even I voted for him – but just that country life makes you more sophisticated. If you grow up in big cities, you end up thinking that places like Hope, Arkansas, are as exotic as Polynesia.

What I don't understand is why everybody is being so touchy about Hillary communicating with Eleanor Roosevelt. I've been talking to Eleanor for years. We chat about everything from housework ('never devote more than 15 minutes a day to it') to politics ('lighting into people never does much good'). The genteel reformer and late First Lady is one of my best friends, and if I can claim any wisdom at all, I have to credit her. Eleanor and I concluded long ago that 'behind every great woman is a man hogging the limelight'.

But it just shows you how far Hillary has come, because communicating with the dead is really a country thing. In the country, death is a way of life. This morning I found one of my Shetland lambs, her soft brown body still warm, strangled on a piece of wire fencing. Someone had turned off the battery connected to the electric netting that protects them from the wire. Last week a fox killed Phoebe, my beloved, immaculately maternal peahen. She had been sitting on five eggs underneath the hornbeam hedge. All we found was a souvenir pile of feathers which we've put in the kitchen window, a kind of make-shift altar to her memory. I miss her and every night this week I've gone out looking for the fox. There is murder in my heart.

Another reason country people spend so much time talking to the dead is that there's no one else to talk to. Whole days go by when my only conversations with the living are with folks who work on the farm or in the garden. Even though these people mean the earth to me, sometimes I yearn for a real heart-to-heart about intimate things like love and money, with people who aren't on my payroll.

Place is an important element in these conversations. Although Hillary seems to find the White House all right for her talks, I prefer the hen-house. Even in rural isolation you need privacy. Lately I've been spending hours in the dark warmth, gazing at my broody Welsummer hen called Sugar who is sitting on ten eggs. No one interrupts us. It is in here that I talk to that once most earthbound of women, Colette. Like me she belonged to a land she had left (hers was Burgundy) and she has shared with me the *sagesse* of her country past.

From her I learned to make rustic barometers out of oat grains, taking two awns as long as a shrimp's feelers, and crucifying them onto a card where they turn to the left or the right according to whether it is going to be fine or wet. These cards sit on the hall table and I have heaps more faith in their forecasts than in the BBC.

Simple prudence counsels us to concentrate on the living, that one's dead companions must not outshine one's living friends. But there are aspects of life in the country that it is well to accept – such as spending more money on magazines, higher telephone bills and never seeing a film until it is on video. 'At the back of all tranquillity,' confides my friend Eleanor, 'is true acceptance'.

July 11, 1996

GONE WITH THE WIND

BY the time the Olympics end this summer you may feel like you have lived in Atlanta. I did live there, for two years back in the early 70s, a dreamy lacuna of time when I wasn't sure where I wanted to be, in a place that wasn't sure if it wanted to be a big city or a country town. In our uncertainty we suited each other just fine.

I arrived in Atlanta a few years after I had vowed I would never live in the South again. I found an apartment at 1559 Peachtree Street with high ceilings, wooden floors, no air conditioning and big windows that looked out onto the Jewish Synagogue through a filter of dogwood trees. I paid $100 a month.

I shared the landing with two elderly ladies whose father had fought in the Battle of Atlanta. Weeks passed before I realised that the Austin sisters and I were the only female occupants of the building. Surrounding us was the cream of Atlanta's gay community, an urban utopia of artistic, talented men who had fled the small, bigoted

Georgia towns of their youth. In apartments transformed into stage sets, they lived interesting, cultivated lives. Eventually they became my best friends, supervising my bookish decor, my haircuts, my cooking and my boyfriends. These were halcyon days, before the property developers took over Peachtree Street and before Atlanta's Center for Disease Control traced a strange illness that would soon be known as AIDS.

A gentle peanut farmer called Jimmy Carter was Governor of the state at the time, presiding over a capital city that was growing at the speed of summer lightning. In one decade, Atlanta acquired a major league sports arena, five professional sports teams, a sleek white marble arts center, a world-class international airport, a state-of-the-art rapid transit system, a mindboggling freeway system, the nation's best convention facilities and a more or less integrated school system.

Of course it was still *Gone With the Wind* country, and you could still meet people who had known Margaret Mitchell, whose one and only novel had sold as many copies as the Bible. Miss Augusta Austin, a retired librarian, informed me that 'Peggy Mitchell got it all wrong: the cotton trade had peaked thirty years earlier and Atlanta wasn't the prosperous city she depicted.' Miss Augusta told me where Margaret Mitchell's house had been (1401 Peachtree Street) and where, at the age of 46, she was fatally hit by a car (at Peachtree and 13th Street).

My own connection to *Gone With The Wind* went back a few years, to one of the most talented men to come out of my Mississippi hometown. Will Price went out to Hollywood in the 1930s, married the Irish actress Maureen O'Hara, and became the speech director of *GWTW*, teaching Vivienne Leigh and Clark Gable their southern accents. Like so many southerners, Will had a weakness for water with Bourbon in it, and in the early 1960s, despite the soulful truth that says you cannot, he left Hollywood and came home to Mississippi.

I didn't recognise the look of defeat in his eyes and listened with worshipful devotion to his tales of Hollywood, re-fuelling him with my father's Jack Daniels. By the time he died – I was twelve – we were each other's best friend, and he left me the only precious thing he had left: his bound copy of the shooting script of *Gone With The Wind*. Inscribed inside: 'For Will, who literally shoved the South down our throats. David O. Selznik.'

Margaret Mitchell said that fame was a kind of death. When a city becomes too famous, it kind of outgrows itself, and something in it dies too. As I watch the miraculous achievements of perfectly-trained athletes going for gold, I'll try not to dwell on the thought that the Atlanta I knew is gone with the wind.

July 1997

FALLS THE SHADOW

MOST deals made with the devil are vague events. I have only the foggiest memory of what took place on the morning that Sam was born. I remember the little knitted hat being put on his head to prevent heat loss, before he was placed, puppylike, at my breast. While he was drinking my milk, I was drinking the cup of milky tea given to me by the midwife. Before either of us had quenched our thirst, Sam was put down for Harrow.

In the ecstatic fog of childbirth, a placid calm comes over you. I agreed to things that I might not have agreed to had I been my usual free-born self. While my infant son was still wrapped in blankets stamped 'Property of Hammersmith Hospital', I surrendered his future, swept up by a powerful force called English tradition.

Even in literature, deals made with the devil have always seemed pretty feasible to me because of the hazy distance between agreement and delivery. It's what I call shadow time, because I think that's what T. S. Eliot meant when he wrote: 'Between the idea and the reality, Between the motion and the act, Falls the Shadow.'

This morning, as we drive through a web of rural Suffolk lanes, I have the feeling my shadow time is running out. It is midsummer and the poppies have begun to look like dresses at a rainy garden fête. We are on our way to see one of the prep schools we have in mind for Sam. Between the idea of prep school and the reality is just over one year.

I cannot now honestly claim delayed shock. From the day Sam was fitted with his first pair of Start-Rite shoes, every decision we have made has been based on this extraordinary goal. As the song goes, 'the hip bone's connected to the thigh bone'; in the same way, the nursery school's connected to the pre-prep, the pre-prep's connected to the prep school, and so it goes on, ending up, you hope, where four generations of Carlisles (and two Sam Carlisles) have been educated.

During the first few minutes of our meeting with the headmaster and his wife, I become completely aphasic. I cannot summon up a common language. My husband tells the polite and bewildered couple that I am American. Of course. That explains the little cultural divide between those who accept as a matter of course that eight-year-old boys are better off without their mothers, and those who do not. It does not explain why I seem to have the vocabulary of an Eskimo.

As we tour the school I slowly understand that the next divide is between mother and father. Mamas are interested in beds and cuddly bears; papas are interested in computers and cricket pavilions. I find comfort in the proximity of the school (45 minutes from home), weekly boarding, Wednesday visits and girls. (I believe that boys benefit from the presence of girls although girls don't benefit from boys. Solve that one.) Sam's papa looks at the list of schools the boys and girls go to when they leave here.

Throughout the morning Sam is civil and manly and cool in the face of newness. Only I can see the shyness in his blue eyes. He is fascinated by a rehearsal in which ten boys all play drums. He is thrilled by the technology and design department. Sam believes prep school is a cross between Enid Blyton's *The Island of Adventure* and *Huckleberry Finn*.

I reach out to brush his hair back from his forehead but I'm too late. He's off to the assault course. As he flies in the air on a rope swing I remember the final line: 'Between the conception and the creation, Between the emotion and the response, Falls the Shadow.' For the next 395 days I shall cherish every hour of the shadow.

July 18, 1996

53

PARADISE LOST

MY best friend is worried that I'm becoming the Anita Brookner of the countryside. She detects an air of melancholy that weaves its way through my accounts of country life. 'Fewer dead animals, please,' she urges, 'just cheer up.'

This advice from someone who knows me so well is worrying. It has the sticky feel of truth. My grandmother was always beseeching me to 'write something cheerful for this gloomy old world'. At seven I was writing stories about kidnappers, drug addicts and alcoholics, topics I gleaned from the conversations of grown-ups.

The truth is, rural melancholia starts in childhood, when the great expanse of empty days rolls in front of you like a Suffolk prairie. I'm not so sure it's a bad thing. I worry about children who are recent migrants from big towns because their parents work so hard at occupying them during the summer. I know lots of mothers who arrange for their children to have someone to play with every single day, or at least one activity planned: a trip to Roller World, an excursion to see *The Hunchback of Notre Dame* followed by Chicken McNuggets, sailing lessons, tennis lessons, a day at Pleasurewood Hills. These mothers are depriving their children of one of the unique gifts of a country childhood: boredom, a feeling that is possible only in these precious weeks when you have all the time in the world.

The boredom of childhood produces the first moments of introspection, which in turn leads to real creativity. I don't mean that all children will start writing like the Brothers Grimm or painting like Francis Bacon, but when they aren't provided with entertainment the moment they whine the word 'bored', they are forced to entertain themselves. This can be just digging a hole. The son of one of our tenants spent summers digging an amazing hole in the ground until it looked like the backyard version of the Grand Canyon. He learned diligence, discipline and the reward of hard work (a deeper hole), with no lasting damage to the landscape. I reckon if Jack becomes a philosopher when he grows up, in his beginning was his hole.

My sister and I were more brutal. We spent our summers practising dog torture. Our dogs were our best friends and they loyally endured common, ordinary tortures such as being dressed up in T-shirts and nappies and being forced to drink milk from old baby bottles.

More sophisticated dog tortures, such as the raisin torture, evolved later, and consisted of placing raisins between their toes: the harder they tried to eat these sweet treats, the tighter they squeezed their paws shut.

Our mother was heartless in summer. She locked us out of the house after breakfast, re-admitting us for lunch, then giving us the option of a nap or being locked out again, ignoring our pleas through the screen doors. We now live in an age where we have to keep a fearful eye on our children. The two things most of us grew up with – freedom and hunger – are luxuries we cannot easily give to our own children.

Country children will never again know the freedom summers enjoyed by Julian, George, Dick, Anne and Timmy in the Enid Blyton stories my son now craves, the freedom to make friends with mysterious strangers, to go off in boats, explore caves and spend days and days without adults. Nor do they know the joy of yearning, of playing tennis for a whole year with a heavy, half-strung, hand-me-down racket and one precious ball, while saving every hard-earned penny for a new and perfect racket of your own. Yearning cannot be bought, and freedom is the paradise that country children have lost, but the fertilising health of a little boredom is within each parent's gift. At least, that's how it seems here at the Hotel du Lac.

July 25, 1996

THE TURK IN ITALY

THE great cultural event of my summer so far has been the stupendous rainfall we watched at Garsington Opera. Now that the open-air opera house has its vast upturned umbrella, the singers, musicians and audience mercifully stay dry. But, as if triggered by the Rossini overture, this was a deluge of such magnitude and steadfastness that all earthly activity came to a halt. We were transfixed. It was like standing at the roar of Niagara Falls, staring down and hearing your heart say 'jump'.

Not that I have ever been to Niagara Falls. In fact this was my first visit to Garsington although I've been steeped in the literature of the place and its earlier owner, Lady Ottoline Morrell, ever since I bought her two volumes of memoirs nearly 20 years ago. As we climbed up the steep Garsington hill, complete with drowsy cows, grey stone houses and village church, I wasn't sure if I felt that we were arriving at a village in the Apennines or if Ottoline had written that in 1915.

I've always felt wretchedly sorry for Ottoline. There she was, this great, horse-faced woman with a passion for the arts, offering hospitality, refuge, encouragement, support, comfort, food and drink to all those thinkers, painters, talkers and writers, and what did she get in return? Ingratitude the size of the Ritz.

During the rainy interlude, I began a mental roll-call of all the famous ingrates who had benefited from the big heart and big country house of this literary hostess: Lytton Strachey, D. H. Lawrence and his supremely thankless wife, Frieda, the mischievous Virginia Woolf, Bertrand Russell, Roger Fry, Middleton Murray and Katherine Mansfield. Their ingratitude was not the easy, careless variety of the month-old thank-you letter or the slender box of After Eights presented as a token of appreciation for three nights in clean sheets and eight meals. No, theirs was an industry of ingratitude recorded in novels, diaries, memoirs and letters in which they defamed, distorted and ridiculed their generous friend.

By the time the rain stopped and *The Turk in Italy* began in earnest, I was well into my theme of ingratitude. Why, I pondered, is generosity so often rewarded with grievance? Even more compelling, why do writers and artists feel that it is their due to be the beneficiaries of generous hosts, as though some divine order deigns the artist as righteous and deserving?

Frankly, the older I get, the less reverential I feel

towards the artist and the writer. I am equally moved by the creative talents of the hostess and the cook, the carpenter and the gardener, the financial director who collects Pugin and devours new novels, the banker who commissions the modern tapestry, the doctors and lawyers who buy the tickets.

If there is any justice in afterlife to compensate for the gargantuan injustice here on earth, it is at Garsington on a summer evening. Ottoline's Italianate gardens are intact. Delicious interval dinners are served in the long barn, now lined with the panelling from Glyndebourne's old opera house. Indeed, everything Ottoline passionately loved – art, music, beauty and pleasure – is here. She would be delighted with the tradition of free dress rehearsals for local residents and schools and the collections that benefit the Garsington Village Trust.

The creators of Garsington Opera, Leonard and Rosalind Ingrams, are as modest as school teachers. In this they reflect the spirit of Ottoline who once wrote: 'I wish I had more subtlety of brain, to write well and talk well. I have such a slow, calm brain, without charm or brilliance.' On a summer's evening, filled with music, food, wine and the company of friends, it is easy to believe that sympathetic understatement is at the heart of what is best in English country life.

August 1, 1996

ENGLISH ROSE

ONCE upon a time, there was such a thing as an English Rose. Although she could be from Scotland, she was usually English. She had clear eyes, shiny hair, excellent teeth and a single strand of pearls. If everything went according to plan, she ended up with an engagement ring worth less than a Rover but more than a Mini.

Although the English Rose was no dummy, her education was rather less rigorous than the training that might be considered adequate for a pair of gundogs. This meant that although the English Rose worked hard looking after husband, children, home, garden and labradors, as well as organising the fund-raising for the local NSPCC/Red Cross/Arthritis Foundation and running her curtain-making/catering/*trompe l'oeil* fire-screens business, she never actually had a job.

Life for the daughter of the English Rose is different. Emma/Sophie/Philippa went to the village school before going, age 13, to boarding school. Following a gap year in

India/Australia/Peru, she went to university at St Andrews/Durham/Newcastle.

Instead of receiving a string of pearls for her 18th birthday, the daughter was given a car. This is because the mother felt less worried at the prospect of Emma/Sophie/Philippa driving herself home late at night than any of the alternatives.

For Christmas she was given a mobile telephone. 'I feel safer knowing she has it,' says her mother. In her daughter's stocking was a heart-shaped alarm on a rope for the in-between times when she might be running on the lonely tracks on their farm or Putney Heath.

Now Emma/Sophie/Philippa is a junior doctor/ solicitor/BBC producer. Her mother and father are proud of her. But still they worry. They don't care that the sapphire earrings left to her by her grandmother were stolen when her flat was burgled because they are too relieved that their daughter did not walk in when the burglar was there. They are happy that she is doing so well in her career but they worry about the odd hours she works and car parks she walks across late at night.

Emma/Sophie/Philippa's mother knows that her daughter loves her independence, but she hopes she will get married all the same. Among other things, a husband is another layer of protection.

Here in the country my friends with daughters say this has been a summer of fear and there is no reprieve, not even for the young. Do you tell your six-year-old daughter she cannot sleep in a tent with her brothers because every time you see the tent you see Sophie Hook's trusting face smiling at you? Can you let your 13-year-old go off to Tuscany with a schoolfriend whose mother is more nonchalant about her children's whereabouts than you are about yours?

I do not have a daughter but 13-year-old Caroline Dickinson looks like the kind of daughter I would have loved: willowy, quiet, poetic. I generally do not save pictures from newspapers but I have kept by my desk the photograph of seven-year-old Megan Russell in her OshKosh overalls, sitting beside her dog, Lucy. I cannot bear to think of her mother whose last desperate attempts in life would have been to protect her daughters.

At last we live in an era where girls are educated as seriously as boys, and women can enter the workplace confident that they can go to the top. Nowhere is this transformation reflected more clearly than in COUNTRY LIFE'S weekly portraits. Today's young women radiate success confidence and happiness. We don't study their engagement rings: we look to see what they do. But the lesson of the summer of '96 is this: women cannot feel truly free unless they feel safe. This is the alarm on a string that is ticking away in our hearts.

August 8, 1996

THE FUGITIVE

To Whom It Concerns:
I would like to cancel my membership in the Moreton Hall
Health Club. As I have not attended once in the two years
in which I have been a member, I believe it would be
uneconomic to continue. Yrs truly.

THE pulmonary stamina required to post this letter
during the heat of the Olympics would indicate a level of
fitness that Michelle Smith might envy. Which is rather
reassuring because when I had my initial assessment at the
health club conveniently located *en route* to Sainsbury's,
the assessor was astonished that I had the lung capacity to
open my car door and walk across the car park.

Indeed, only under 'agility' did I score higher than an
invalid. I can stand on my head and do splits in the air as
nimbly as a 13-year-old Romanian, but I cannot (will not)
run to the bottom of the drive unless there is a Jacob lamb
about to meet its death in the middle of the road.

I am not proud of my defection from the health club. Confessing it here is a sort of condensed version of the 12-step programme. But there comes a day when £11 a month by direct debit to finance one's dreamy optimism can no longer be considered a bargain.

One of the problems is that going to the gym does not feel like a country thing. In the country we are supposed to stay fit by taking long walks, roguing wild oats, chasing the sheep out of the apple orchard, swimming in rivers, baling hay. Adding a vineyard to your endeavours – all that bending in the hot sun, all that worry about costs – is the rural equivalent of acquiring a personal trainer.

Still, I don't look like the woman who strode across the fields as a bride ten years ago. As the French philosopher Roland Barthes said: 'the only thing at stake is your image of yourself'. The problem is, my image of myself is Julie Christie struggling to make something grow in the Siberian kitchen garden in *Dr Zhivago*, not Farmer Hogget's wife in *Babe*. If the road to my bonier past meant operating machines in a crowded, sweaty room, this seemed a sacrifice that had to be made.

Sadly, my real life is that of the farmer's wife. I am much too busy rushing about to ride a bicycle that goes nowhere. Nor do I crave the companionship that entices some people to join a health club. I never see enough of the friends I already have and when I do, I want to sit down and talk over a glass of wine, not be speechless with effort and pain.

What does seem to be a country thing are slimming clubs such as Weight Watchers and Slimmers World. One of my skinniest friends persuaded me to join her in the primary school in Walsham-le-Willows one evening at one of these meetings.

After a lengthy roll call of members who were publically weighed and their success or failure broadcast to loud applause or hearty commiseration, I got to come forward and stand on the scale. Until that moment I had felt like an interloper and was rather embarrassed for the roomful of Farmer Hogget wifelets. Then I was told that I should reckon on three months (the gradual approach) to get down to my ideal weight. I felt like I had been caught with vodka in my coffee cup.

Of course I never went back. Somewhere in my museum of diet books I have their literature. But from the £264 I paid to the health club I learned a lesson for life that I will give to you, dear reader, absolutely free: never join anything until you have been three times. Meanwhile, I'm going on the only regime I know that makes me feel great all the time: fried green tomatoes, corn bread, iced tea, and a little meditation in the shade.

August 15, 1996

II
Flowering

HARVEST MOON

CELEBRATING my tenth wedding anniversary in Southwold was truly something I never thought I would do. For a start, I never thought I would be married so long. Okay. I never thought I would get married at all. Ever since I read Margaret Kennedy's *The Constant Nymph* when I was 12, I saw myself living alone in a rambling house in England, wearing black stockings and growing mushrooms in the cellar. I also saw myself reading books all day long. I never, ever saw myself in supermarket aisles or waiting for a husband to come in the door, take one sniff and say 'Yummy, fish pie'.

Even after I had acquired the little flat in the rambling house in Putney and enough extra-soft, opaque black tights from Marks & Spencer to supply a remake of *Zorba the Greek*, there was no husband in my dreams. By then I had also eliminated mushrooms from my plans, having read a book on fungi composting that rather put me off suburban agriculture.

But then the day came and I met Mr Right. Even now he thinks it was merely by chance we were both at Jane's for dinner that night in Battersea. Believe me, the planning was as tricky as the Normandy invasion. The attentive and amused look on my face as we chatted over the kedgeree was worthy of Katherine Hepburn. I had learned every detail of his life since birth long before I picked up my fork.

My own mother and father were so sceptical about my wedding plans that they were unable to get Apex tickets. They didn't even call the airlines until they received the engraved invitation. 'She's done a lot of things,' said my pa holding it up to the light, 'but this is the first one of these.'

Only my grandmother was disappointed. Not because I was getting married but because I was marrying a farmer and a politician. This is what she had done nearly 60 years earlier and she warned me: 'He'll have a grand life but you will get stuck on the farm.' She was right, and I already knew from my childhood that farms are hard places to get away from.

What I did not realise on that hot day at the end of July ten years ago was that my wedding day was also the beginning of harvest. The harvests of my childhood were at the proper harvest time: September. So our *lune de miel* consisted of three days in the Isles of Scilly ('a botanist's paradise') before rushing home to the harvest.

In the intervening decade I thought my beloved had

learned a thing or two. That I'm too myopic to appreciate botany and that I prefer a wine lover's/music-lover's/food-lover's paradise. That the hourly telephone calls checking on the nitrogen levels of the malting barley interrupt the conversational flow. That the progress reports on the new New Holland combine harvester do not mean as much to me as the new volume of Seamus Heaney poems.

Which is not to say that I don't love being in the combine myself gliding across the fields, watching the hares do Carl Lewis impressions as their cover of barley disappears. Behind the control panel I feel like Amelia Earhart. The ice-cold air-conditioning feels as soothing to me as an expensive restaurant. And then there's the music. I have my own combine harvester tapes: a little Boccherini to get started, followed by the Everly Brothers singing *Sleepless Nights,* and *He's a Rebel* by the Crystals. If the farm manager signals that I'm going too fast I slow down to Elgar's Cello Concerto.

Maybe it's what happens when you are married for ten years. You drive to another part of Suffolk and check into the Swan at Southwold. You celebrate your good romantic luck with champagne for lunch and for dinner. And the next day you get back to the harvest. It feels all right. In fact, it feels like a honeymoon.

August 22, 1996

A COMRADE'S FAREWELL

WHEN I heard that Jessica Mitford had died a few weeks ago I felt the sudden loneliness you feel when you lose a treasured friend. I also felt sad that my souvenirs of that friendship had not survived. Being a vagabond has its drawbacks.

The archives that most people keep – newspaper clippings, photographs, love letters – rarely survive the soulful reappraisals that accompany each move. Now I have roots and an acre of attics but the shoeboxes of memory are mostly in my mind.

I no longer have the yellowed photograph from the *San Francisco Chronicle* that records our first meeting in August 1969. We are standing there with Bernadette Devlin who has addressed an audience of longshoremen. I have just graduated from college and gone out to California to save the world and I'm embarrassed, not at appearing alongside Bernadette Devlin but because I think Jessica Mitford looks a bit tweedy. By then she had lived in America for 30 years, but she sounded and looked as English to me as Margaret Rutherford. She certainly didn't look like my idea of a comrade-in-arms.

It was not until years later, when I read *Hons and Rebels*, that I began to understand how remarkable she was.

'Growing up in the English countryside seemed an interminable process,' she wrote in her memoir. 'Freezing winter gave way to frosty spring, which in turn merged into chilly summer – but nothing ever, ever happened!'

Insert 'hot', 'hotter' and 'sick hot' for 'freezing', 'frosty', and 'chilly' in that passage and it could be 18 miles from Greenwood, Mississippi. *Hons and Rebels* contributed to my theory about radical politics. It may not hold up to close examination, but here it is. Being marooned in a country childhood sets you up for feeling life passionately later on. Years of nothing ever, ever happening seem bound to lead you to a life that is more complex, less reasonable, more desperate.

For Jessica Mitford, known to her family and friends as Decca, this meant running away from home, eloping with her cousin Esmond Romilly, and fighting (well, nearly) in the Spanish Civil War. Of her five other sisters, one became a Nazi, one a Fascist, one a pragmatic, country-loving duchess and one merely a famous novelist.

I'm not saying those were not tumultuous times. In the late 1930s the whole world was in turmoil. But my belief is that, out of the isolation of their childhood, the

Mitfords acquired that funny mix of wild innocence and dumb confidence that makes you believe you can change the world.

Decca believed that by fighting with the International Brigade in Spain she would stop Fascism in its tracks. After she had fled to America she believed that by becoming a Communist she could end the evils of capitalism and injustice.

My childhood was less exotic and less eccentric. Still, while my sister was Miss Mississippi and gliding down the ramp at the Miss America pageant, I was planning my programme to integrate the all-white churches in my state. In my family, as in Decca's, there were long periods when it was hard to keep track of who was 'on speakers' with whom.

Like Decca, I found that a sense of humour was not highly prized among the comrades. A love of food and wine was equally suspect. We both found that swapping countries helped us to live with our views of the world and that, in the end, dogma was like an overcoat that is too heavy to wear indoors.

Thirty years on I think a red-hot radical would find me embarrassingly tweedy. I just hope I will wear my tweeds with the same humane wit and warmth that was Decca's all the days of her life.

August 29, 1996

THE FLIGHT PATH

'As a man packeth, so shall ye know him.' Or 'From each according to his ability, to each according to his suitcase.' In a few hours we leave for our family vacation. No one is packed. Rather, no one is fully packed. A miracle of consolidation is required before we load the car and head for the airport.

Most people we know plan their holidays with the grace and precision of a Chopin waltz. Even as I write, we know families who are white-water rafting in Idaho, journeying by train to St Petersburg, riding western on estancias in Chile and family bonding in the Amazon jungle. Not the Carlisle family.

For a start, we cannot agree on who should be travel planner. We both have forfeited the role through earlier failures. My husband has a weakness for the bleak. His idea of heaven is the Isle of Lewis, where we spent two weeks a couple of summers ago on a fishing estate owned by his oldest friend.

The lunar nature of the island was so pervasive that I am convinced I saw a stainless steel plaque reading: 'Here men from planet Earth first set foot upon the moon, July AD 1969. We came in peace for all mankind.' My husband claims that it was a visitor information sign paid for by the European Union.

When Sam was four I planned our holiday in Virginia. We stayed in Holiday Inns with swimming pools for $68 a night, ate at the Red Lobster and the Pancake House, and wandered round Civil War battlefields. I thought it was perfect. The problem was the heat: 104°F by noon most days.

So now nobody wants to take the responsibility which, in travel language, is just another word for blame.

This year I wanted to spend two weeks in August at Monteagle, Tennessee, where I spent my childhood summers. A community of rambling Victorian houses in the Cumberland mountains, Monteagle was built at the turn of the century by folk from Mississippi and Alabama wanting to escape the yellow fever. Our family saying, announced at the end of each summer, was: 'We had a great time: nobody got hurt.'

Which was rarely the case. When so many emotional Southerners are gathered in one place, somebody's feelings are always getting hurt. In any case, I concluded that my husband might not find a two-week family reunion so peaceful.

Then I heard Seamus Heaney reading from *The Spirit Level* on Radio 4. 'Ireland,' I said longingly. Out came the maps and my husband's eyes went straight to the empty coastlines beyond Connemara. I focused on areas where people are known to live, before scanning those little boxes in the Saturday *Telegraph:* 'Luxury self-catering cottages set in 45 acres of glorious countryside. Close to Cork.'

It was that little word luxury I liked (translated, it means sheets and towels provided) and the thought of being four miles from the sea and within easy reach of pubs, music, restaurants and shops. When you live in the middle of nowhere, being somewhere is a holiday.

Yesterday, each member of this little family packed their version of *Desert Island Discs*. Sam has his Walkman, story tapes, Enid Blyton books and a new Game Boy. My husband has botanical guides to Ireland, binoculars and rain gear, Roy Jenkins's life of Gladstone and Robert Kee's *Parnell*.

What have I packed? Four silver forks and hefty knives, four napkins large enough to sail a small boat, a pepper mill, Maldon salt, olive oil, balsamic vinegar and a chunk of Parmesan Regianno the size of a man's foot. My cashmere socks. And for the joy of brooding, *The Spirit Level*. As I go to wake the others, I think of Heaney's line from *The Flight Path*: 'Skies change, not cares, for those who cross the seas.'

September 5, 1996

THE NEW ASCENDANCY

'Who'd want to ride over this country now, the place is like a birdcage. There should be no wire on a gentleman's estate... except on a champagne bottle, and that ought to be ready to come off at a moment's notice.'

WHEN I first came across those words by the late Molly Keane, she was resting under the pseudonym 'M. J. Farrell' and I was *en route* to Ireland to write about a hunt breakfast for an American magazine. The host of the lawn meet was J. P. Donleavy, an American writer who had long made his home in Ireland, a wise and cautious man who does not himself hunt. Unlike the beautiful young Mrs Donleavy: a glamourous figure on a hunter, complete with tight white breeches, high boots, hair pulled hack in a net and tucked under her bowler hat. Although I would have to do a major rewrite on the piece – my editor felt my first version made the wife appear too 'bloodless' – I thought the (then) Mrs Donleavy was pretty amazing for a girl from Baltimore.

In fact it was a story that needed the latitude of a novel, not the restraints of a lifestyle piece with peat fires in Adam fireplaces, angels on horseback (the kind made with plump Galway oysters), the origin of the term 'Pink coat', and the handsome Master of the Westmeath Hunt demonstrating the long, tricky process of drawing a glass of dark, creamy Guinness.

I was rather overcome at just being there. I felt that I was glimpsing the Anglo-Irish world in its amber glow, not just witnessing an ersatz re-creation of those long-gone days when the gentry passed six days in the week hunting while their houses picturesquely decayed and the countryside deteriorated. So utterly did I feel like a member of the house party that I forgot about my readers who also expected me to provide recipes for soda bread and Guinness stew.

Fifteen years later I'm not sure I could fool myself so easily. I've come back to an Ireland that has changed more in one fat decade than in the long century of twilight captured in the Irish memories of Molly Keane. I can't think what she would make of the new Ascendancy, the European Union: omnipresent, all-powerful, all-generous, its flag of deep blue and circle of gold stars flying above the airport at Cork, engraved on every car licence plate and proclaimed on billboards throughout the land.

The old Ascendancy believed Land was Power. It took

a couple of hundred years, but in the end they were proved wrong. The new Ascendancy believe that Roads are Power. Nearly all of the £3 billion the EU pours into Ireland each year is spent on smoothing and straightening, widening and dividing the roads – the same roads that were mostly built by the old Ascendancy. The EU is bursting with the desire to exploit Ireland's strong and attractive character, to develop it and to lure more people to it. There is a restlessness in the air, a kind of bewilderment, and the highest growth rate in Europe.

Don't get me wrong. I'm not so heartless that I yearn for Ireland to freeze in time so that each village is as bleak as a William Trevor short story, each dilapidated Georgian house a stage set of terrible snobberies and decay. It's simply that I believe that Ireland is one of the last real places left.

Maybe it doesn't matter that the new 'birdcage' over the place will be four-lane highways across the land. The he-and-the-she of it is that the Irish are as proud of their new roads as they are tickled with the EU. Maybe I, a mere visitor, cannot understand that Irishness runs so deep that straightening up roads which meander nowhere will not change Ireland for ever. Maybe it doesn't matter that Ireland's future is beginning to look an awful lot like our past.

September 12, 1996

NOBLE DOG

THE kitchen bed and the upstairs bed are in the cellar. The pillows, blankets and faded quilts that cushioned the arthritic hips have been through the washing machine. The bowls with their Gitane blue glaze are in the back larder.

Still, when I come through the kitchen door I expect to see him slowly unfolding himself, rising like a gentleman of the old school. I look for the smile that asks: 'Did you miss me as much as I missed you?'

To outsiders Adam probably seemed a polite but ordinary labrador. He may have amused garden visitors witnessing his morning stroll to the apple orchard and his skillful selection of the best windfall. More gatherer than hunter, he chose the ripest pears off low, gnarled branches and munched strawberries in the kitchen garden.

Adam would have been an excellent candidate for *This Is Your Life*. He survived a genuine kidnapping from Putney Heath when he was only three months old (miraculously returned after three weeks); a dive from a rocky cliff into the sea where I was swimming in Cornwall; a night in the Bury St Edmunds gaol after a late-in-life romantic quest; persecution from a self-made cat who would become his closest companion. Adam did not bring me to England but he and quarantine laws kept me here. For him I gave up a much-loved house in Burgundy and then a country. When I married, Adam was my dowry and my husband's first dog.

But my loyalty was not always steadfast. The day we brought Sam home from hospital I shrieked 'dog germs', and ignored his hurt looks. My husband sided with Adam in this new distribution of love and they went for long walks together, returning bewildered but forgiving. Eventually, the maternal witch disappeared and only dog and only child became best friends.

At the time in life when most dogs start thinking about retirement, Adam took a day job. This meant spending his summers stretched across the open doorway of the vineyard restaurant, his winters hogging the wood-burning stoves. He greeted customers, pacified fretful babies, amused restless children, and for four years eluded the critical eye of every health inspector.

X-rays foretold the hip dysplasia that stalks his breed. One day Adam reluctantly resigned from the vineyard walk. He looked so forlorn when we left him behind that I too gave up walking and took to driving us the short half mile. Then one evening he sat at the bottom of the stairs, informing me with sad eyes that his stair-climbing days were over. I picked him up, all four stone, and carried him up the stairs. This would he his mode of transport every night for the last two years of his life.

My father wrote: 'Adam needs a living will.' And I agreed: when he could no longer manage the short stroll from the house to the barn.

Adam was a birthday present 14 years ago and every year we celebrate together. Last week as we ambled to the restaurant, he sank into the grass like a seal on a rock. He could go no farther. The next morning we carried him out to the apple orchard. While we were waiting for the vet, Sam became an anguished one-child ethics committee: 'Would you put me to sleep just because I couldn't walk?'

Adam relished the breakfast in his honour: ripe Brie, oatmeal cookies and carrots. Somehow he snuffled his way towards a Beauty of Bath, our earliest-ripening apple. He ate it with pure pleasure.

While we cradled Adam in our arms, the young Australian vet explained what would happen. We wept as he searched for the crucial vein.

The line between a dog's long life and death is a mere 30 seconds. In our Wyken graveyard is buried the friend who gave me roots and shared nearly a third of my life. Thank you, good dog.

September 19, 1996

COMMON PRAYER

IT'S been a quiet week here at Wyken. Sam's gone back to school, the harvest is finished and now we're waiting for the drilling to begin.

It's at peaceful times like this that folk on the farm start getting on each other's nerves. It comes out each morning at coffee time. For five years now the farm has been sharply divided between those who feel sorry for Diana, those who feel sorry for Charles, and the ones who are fed up with both. It got so bad after *Panorama* that the pair of them became a forbidden subject round the kitchen table at break time.

It seemed strange to me because the forbidden topics round the dinner table when I was growing up were more general: snakes, politics and religion.

Snakes were the most obvious taboo because once you start telling snake stories you can't stop. As children we craved tales of deadly water moccasins wrapping round boat paddles, and friendly king snakes crawling into the house through the bath plughole. Even now I make Sam wear his high-top Doc Martens when he picks blackberries, although rattlesnakes are rare in the blackberry bushes of Suffolk.

Politics was out because my grandfather, the county prosecuting attorney, believed that a society that outlawed a glass of Bourbon in the cool of the evening on your own front porch, but sanctioned hanging, was on the dark edge of civilisation. He was out of step with his times.

He was even further out when it came to religion. A radical Darwinian who did not believe in the Resurrection, it was his bad luck to have four brothers who were Baptist preachers. Papa (pronounced Paw-Paw) loved hymns and spirituals, and cried at christenings, weddings and funerals, but he thought the doctrine of Hell was a terrible flaw in the Christian belief.

That may be why my own parents became high church Episcopalians: Hell didn't seem to apply to us. Although the Baptists and Methodists had all the best hymns, we drank real wine at Communion, got dots on our foreheads on Ash Wednesday and burned incense at Christmas.

My cousins and I were filled with the sweetness and cruelty of Christianity. We played Communion with Welch's grape juice and goldfish food. We wore sheets and crowns of thorns and baptised each other and all our dogs. Our every service included a rendition of the opening words of Psalm 137: 'By the rivers of Babylon, there we sat down, yea, we wept, when we remembered Zion.' Then we cried real tears as Zion was the name of our faithful mule who had died in front of our very eyes.

The grim end of that Psalm caused us to tremble: 'Blessed shall he be that takest thy little ones and dashest them against the stone.'

Which brings me to Prince Charles and his so-called disenchantment with the Church of England. I reckon he is not alone.

Maybe this farm isn't typical but we have our share of people who used to cut the grass in the churchyard, repair the banners of the Mothers' Union and generally enjoy the Christian religion and services of the Church of England. The language of the *Book of Common Prayer* may not thrill them but the cadence is in their memory.

But come Sunday nowadays they don't go to church. They work in their gardens, read the newspapers, play bowls, walk the dogs across the fields and have a family meal. Their reverence for the holiness of life seems less and less at home with organised religion.

I wonder if their disenchantment is all that surprising. My grandfather believed that the church would always decline if people got the idea that their fate was not in the hands of God but in the hands of the state. But that's a case of politics butting into religion which really is like stepping on a snake.

September 26, 1996

CITY LIGHTS

IT is a truth not universally acknowledged that if you live in the country, and are blessed with a school run through potato fields that spread out like an infinity of possibility, much of your life will be spent in idle speculation.

It is on the solo stretch, homeward bound, that these thoughts are at their most exploratory and extended. What triggers these aimless meanderings is usually so slender, so effervescent – the wan little boy who is always brought to school by his father, a plea from your child to make something from scratch for the school bake sale – that they will evaporate the moment you drive through the Tesco car wash or see the milk bottles left on the breakfast table.

Every once in a while, however, the speculation becomes dangerously subversive. When, despite everything, one's thoughts turn to city life. For here is another unacknowledged truth: if your life is spent in front of your dark green, double-oven Aga, the last thing you yearn for is an Aga saga.

The *agents provocateurs* of these mental excursions are almost always one's unmarried London friends who are so pleased that you are settled in the country. You provide the perfect setting for a weekend (intimate but relaxed) in the early stages of a love affair ('what do you think?') and a haven for comfort at the tail end of a luckless love affair. (That is what I thought.)

These friends arrive wearing clothes in the size I was before I married, and bearing Diptyque candles and cheeses from Jeroboams. They also bring morsels of gossip as light as *biscotti*, and sometimes the words lodge in my mind like a flint inside a wellington boot.

'So after they had been lovers for a few weeks, he said he wanted to give her three accounts. Wherever she liked. Where do you think she chose?' Henrietta asks while I stir the pumpkin risotto.

My mind is dumbed by rural and domestic life. I cannot think of anywhere more desirable and crucial than Peter Jones. Henrietta looks at me pityingly. Then, as though speaking to a foreigner, she says: 'Pulbrook & Gould. Heywood Hill. A black taxi cab account.'

Oh, the poetry of those words. I am mesmerised by this woman's urbane and scrupulous choices: Heywood Hill in Curzon Street, that most genteel and literary of bookshops, offering new and old books, conveniently located near the London Library and Fortnums. Pulbrook & Gould, the elegant flower shop off Sloane Square. Black

London taxis on call and account, a guarantee of safety and sanity whatever the hour or weather. She is my perfect heroine: modest, meticulous, literary, correct.

As I gather mouldy windfalls I can almost smell the pots of hothouse gardenias in her sitting room. I watch as she unwraps the books on her desk. I see her having lunch in the Tate Gallery restaurant, I thrill to the Stravinsky-esque squeal of taxi brakes as she returns home.

While I load the back of the Volvo with loo paper, cat food and light bulbs, I imagine my heroine at the movies with friends and eating Chinese takeaway afterwards. The thought of waxy white cartons with little wire handles makes me as wistful as friends in Battersea feel about fields of Suffolk poppies.

Only recently have I begun to understand what the English born and bred have always understood: that the true history of this country is to be found in the momentum created by these mutual and opposite longings. Those who live in the countryside dream of city life; city-dwellers dream of apple orchards, Michaelmas daisies and boot rooms. I am surrounded by fields ploughed by the Romans and woodlands older than Robin Hood, and I am grateful. Still, tonight I think I'll watch the video of *Sunday, Bloody Sunday*, accompanied by Marks & Spencer Peking duck.

October 10, 1996

THE RIGHTS OF DOGS

MY father has just called to tell me his travel arrangements for Christmas. He arrives at Gatwick, will stay a month, and would he grateful if I could have the shower installed by the time he arrives.

My father: scholarly, indolent, and a grudging Anglophile. He has never forgiven the English for that maddening plan to impose taxation on the colonies without any form of representation. He likes his cup of Darjeeling in the afternoon and scoffs at the English who put milk in their tea. He smiles when he thinks about all that tea in Boston Harbour.

Pa thinks the war of 1812 against the British was perfectly just. He deplores Palmerston's insolence to Lincoln.

But there is one Englishman he admires with all his heart: Thomas Paine. When he came over last October his one desire was to visit Thetford, the Norfolk town ten miles from us and the birthplace of Tom Paine.

Personally I find Thetford a little bleak but my father saw the charm in the flint buildings and timber-frame houses. As he stood in front of the statue of Paine presented to Thetford by the Thomas Paine Society of the United States, I saw tears in his eyes.

'They didn't even want it. The burghers of Thetford believed he was a traitor to his country. But he was never a traitor to humanity.'

My father still holds a grudge against William Cobbett for bringing Paine's remains hack to England. 'Tom Paine died and was buried on his farm in New York, the land given to him out of gratitude by the States after the war. That's where he should have stayed.'

Although I reckon he knows by heart *The Rights of Man* in which Paine advocated a revolution in Britain, these days Pa has a new cause. He is agitated by the rights of dogs. More particularly, by the rights of dogs in Britain. He takes it personally. If Britain didn't have its 75-year-old quarantine laws, he could bring his dog and spend three months a year in Suffolk with his daughter who married an Englishman.

He also feels it on a deeper level. He is horrified by what happened to Mr Bogie, the 12-year-old cocker spaniel belonging to a Danish diplomat. In June, Mr Bogie was put in a licensed kennel in West Sussex for six months where he was confined to a small space with concrete floors and draughts.

Three months later Mr Bogie died. His family was never told he had been ill. Although the kennel said it was liver cancer, the owners were not allowed to see Mr Bogie's body or order an autopsy. All they were given was a Tesco bag containing a Nescafé jar filled with ashes.

My father thinks the quarantine laws reflect the insularity and paranoia of an 'island mentality'. He sends me articles in which the Government admits that only one of the 200,000 animals put in quarantine in the past 25 years may have been infected with rabies before it arrived, while hundreds of animals die in – or soon after they are released from – quarantine. He calls the quarantine Kennel Owners' Association an extortionate private prison service.

'Hey, we aren't talking Nelson Mandela here,' I say. But in my heart I think he's right.

Dogs in the US are required by law to have a rabies vaccination every three years. The jingle jangle of greeting from every American dog comes from the address tags and rabies date tags attached to their collars. It's not that rabies doesn't exist, but simply that you can control it with the vaccine.

Meanwhile, Pa is writing a pamphlet on the subject, using one of Tom Paine's titles – *Common Sense*. It begins with Paine's most celebrated line: 'These are the times that try men's souls'.

October 17, 1996

WEEKEND TWILIGHT

THOREAU, naturalist and country lover, put it like this: *'The art of life, of a poet's life, is, not having anything to do, to do something.'* I'd put it this way: 'The art of life, of country life, is, not having to invite anyone, to invite people to come and stay.'

Now it gets tricky. I don't want my friends to get the idea that I do not welcome the challenge of clean sheets and fresh towels. I would be genuinely sorry if my guests felt that I am not content to see that the two top drawers are empty (although Americans do not unpack their drawer-size things); that virgin soaps reside on basin and bath; that six empty hangers dangle in the cupboard; that gently sparkling Hildon water is on the table, alongside flowers from the garden and several dozen back copies of COUNTRY LIFE – just in case they don't know that the pressure of words sometimes eats into my natural hospitality.

Please understand: I love filling this house with friends

and family. You don't have to be a Bolshevik to feel that nine bedrooms divided between three people, two of whom share, is not the way things ought to be. When I married I embarked on the transformation of the guest rooms with the zeal of a freedom fighter. I replaced box springs and mattresses in the belief that nothing ensures good behaviour like a comfortable bed. I invested in a pillow programme which guarantees each guest at least one goosedown pillow, and a second pillow for propping up. I installed lamps with 100 watt bulbs so that everyone could read in bed.

To the grief of my mother-in-law, I removed the basins installed in the fifties as I think they are an eyesore in bedrooms. Because I do not sit gazing into a three-panelled mirror, brushing my hair and dabbing Guerlain's *l'Heure Bleue* behind my ears, I scrapped dressing tables in favour of writing tables. Friends who arrive with their laptops welcome the change. For those with *Chanel No 5* and loose powder this is baffling.

Yet all this is only the stage set for a country weekend which must be fuelled with good food and wine as well as planned activity. And here I fall down. In the beginning I spent my Fridays shopping as though preparing for a siege. I then spent the weekend cooking. The structure of the weekend revolves round three major meals – Friday evening, Saturday evening and Sunday lunch. Like a character in *Noises Off,* as soon as dinner was edible, I raced upstairs and changed into my black cashmere V-neck (Friday) or my grandmother's Jean Patou bias-cut tea gown (Saturday). I then strolled into the hall as though I'd been lingering at my dressing-table while my guests drank champagne and Cook deglazed the pan.

Now, however, the fast-cooking, quick-change artist does all this rather less. As does my sister-in-law Christabel, my most gracious friend Arabella, and my blue-stocking friend Helen. Between us we represent a mere 42 bedrooms, but I believe a study of our habits and attitudes might conclude that we are in the twilight of the country-house weekend. For here is the hard sociological truth: men long for rooms to be filled with flowers, candlelight, conversation and bodies. Women do not.

Once upon a time in the large country house, entertaining was a lady's principal occupation. Now women who live in large houses also run their own international design practice, work on MAs, lecture on rain forest renewal.

I may be wrong. Smythson continues to produce visitors' books (bound in buffalo grain leather, 8in by 11in, £149, house name printed in deep gold letters, the words Visitors' Book nowhere to be seen.) It's simply that I have the feeling that few of the hosts – and hostesses – will ever see the pages filled from beginning to end.

October 24, 1996

SMALL IS BEAUTIFUL

THE 7lb sugar beet nestles on the altar like a pig's head without its cherry. Its smiling snout looks as sweet as Babe sleeping in the autumn sun. Alongside it is a Tate & Lyle 1lb bag of caster sugar, in case anyone is curious about just how much sugar a 7lb sugar beet yields. (You calculate 17% of the beet's weight.) Sam astonished us when he pulled the giant specimen out of the tough, dry earth as we walked across the fields on Sunday afternoon. Getting it home was like carrying a big baby without a sling.

Also on the altar, tucked among pumpkins, leeks, tins of peas and Hovis loaves, is a bottle of Wyken wine and two and a half bunches of grapes. That's how many grapes it takes to make a bottle of wine. And this is what we are harvesting on the farm now: sugar beet and grapes.

It's a tense and worrisome time. Everybody wants something different. I want Indian summer days so that the grapes can become ripe enough to make into wine. My husband wants rain so that the newly drilled winter wheat and barley will germinate. This nerve-wracking conflict of interests seems peculiarly at odds with the soft soprano voices.

We plough the fields and scatter the good seed on the land.

The harvest service at Sam's school takes place in a small Victorian church that once was the spiritual heart of a large agricultural estate. Now it is a Betjeman-esque jewel among the functional buildings on a 100-acre campus. Instead of farmworkers, the church is filled with teachers and parents whose principal crop sings to us.

We thank you Lord for those who drive, To bring us food where we can buy.

Here in the heart of the countryside, few of these children are farm children. Sons and daughters of Toyota dealers and estate agents, harvest for them means leaving for school ten minutes earlier from now until February, as the lorries and tractor-trailers hauling beet into the sugar factory clog country roads for a radius of 40 miles. Not that these children don't have country antennae: they know that when you can smell the sweet, burnt-sugar smell emanating from the factory chimneys it usually means rain.

The sermon is aimed at the five-year-olds' attention span. I gaze at the children, thinking that the title from the late E. F. Schumacher's book *Small is Beautiful* applies to their faces. There is not one child here who isn't appealing, sweet to look at, huggable.

My mind wanders to what Schumacher wrote about farming, about how the management of our land should be oriented towards three goals: health, beauty and permanence. Food then comes naturally from it.

Although half the mothers sitting here will probably stop at Tesco or Sainsbury's after this service, we all worry about the health of the land. Even when we don't have time to think about it, we still worry about the beef, chicken, sausages, beans and potatoes our children are eating. We are surrounded by meticulous fields but every day the production of our food seems more remote.

This is harvest festival and here sits a farmer who feels no pride at the harvest of Eurocrops and the weeds of set-aside. That sigh of relief when the set-aside cheque arrives means that now it feels like a paycheck. What I yearn for is a Common Agricultural Policy which subsidises only the health of the land and the creatures that live on it; that restricts phosphate fertilisers; that locks large corporations out of the subsidy system altogether; that supports the farmer whose chickens and pigs and cows roam about.

As we sing our harvest song, clear and joyful, loud and strong, Help us, Father, now to see...

October 31, 1996

WINE SNOBS

THIS is one of those days when I feel really good about the greenhouse effect. Although I deeply regret that I failed to buy shares in Beach Baby sunblock or invest my egg money in the water industry, I like to think I showed prophetic entrepreneurial flair back in 1988, by planting seven acres of vines on a south-facing slope in a country known for its rain.

At least, that is how I feel today. By 10am the thermometer on the vineyard tool shed was bang on 70°F and I'd stripped down to my 'Just Do It' T-shirt and John Deere cap. This is the sunny side of the street and the pickers have been getting a heaped 20lb bucket of grapes off every vine. And not just quantity, but great grapes: clean and ripe, a variety called Bacchus that wins all our medals and has the whiff of cat peewee that Jancis Robinson prizes in *Sauvignon Blanc*.

By 3:15pm, when I have to go and collect Sam from school, my hands are stiff with sticky, sweet grape juice and my back stiff from bending over. We have picked nearly four tonnes, from a section of the vineyard which is just one-and-a-half acres.

My child is too nice to pretend he doesn't know me when I arrive at his school looking as though I've just stepped out of *The Grapes of Wrath*, but on his behalf I ditch my cap and put on the L. L. Bean jacket that lives in the car for just such an emergency. Still, I long to swagger up to the shy cluster of waiting mothers and say: 'Four tonnes of Bacchus, 4,000 bottles. Whoopee!' Instead, I just smile and say hello, and they smile back politely and look down at my sticky boots. It is still 70°F outside.

The truth is, we may be sandy loam over chalk with a microclimate from heaven, but the Napa Valley we are not. Viticulture is not part of Suffolk culture. To plant a vineyard in England, you have to have deep, masochistic needs that cannot be met by other legal means, or possess such dreamy optimism that reality can't touch you. We fell into the latter category with extenuating circumstances: our south-facing slope burned up the sugar beet in a hot summer, and I felt homesick for the vineyards of my past.

More important, I was convinced we could make good wine. Like English apples that stay on the tree longer than French apples, developing crisp, intense appley flavours, English grapes spend longer on the vine producing crisp, flavourful wines. There are a lot of beautiful English wines out there, from vineyards such as Northbrook Springs, Shawsgate, Breaky Bottom and Penshurst.

Still, for everything in its favour, there are ten things going against English wine. Such as the price. Everyone complains that English wines are expensive, but the Government requires English producers to pay the same high taxes as on any imported wine – £1.05 a bottle, which represents excise duty plus the VAT on that duty – a tax on the tax. When we plead for a bit of help against the imported wines, such as being able to sell our wines at the vineyard gate free of tax as the French and Germans do, we are told that this is against EU law.

But much as I enjoy buckin' and snortin' about the Government's unhelpful attitude (and I have never, ever been served an English wine at No 10, No 11 or No 12 Downing Street) I'm afraid the real blame belongs elsewhere. The problem with English wine is that it is considered rather non-U, like 'serviette', 'toilet' and 'phone'. The English are just plain snobbish about English wine.

But I reckon you are going to have to get over that. The weather scientists say that East Anglia will be the new Loire before the Millennium. It's a shame about all those *appellation controllée* vines being replaced with sugar cane, but once you get the hang of it, I think you'll enjoy your travels in Suffolk along the wine route.

November 7, 1996

DOG DAYS

YOU can go a long time without knowing what people think about you. If you do find out, the revelations will probably come about by chance. All week long I have been searching for a labrador puppy. There are three schools of thought here. One is the Gertrude Stein school wherein you acquire a new dog within days, if not hours, after the old dog dies. Alice B. Toklas and Gertrude Stein had a white standard poodle called Basket. When Basket died they got a new white standard poodle whom they named Basket. As Miss Stein nearly said, a dog is a dog is a dog.

Then there is the 'Old Yeller' school in which you get a puppy just as the mature dog begins to take short cuts on walks. The theory here is that the young dog will rejuvenate the old dog as well as dilute your grief when the sad day comes.

But I personally subscribe to the Queen Victoria school of High Mourning. Here the twilight years of old dog are spent in only-dog serenity, unblighted by an ear-chewing puppy who constantly competes for affection, bed space and Winalot. Naturally, when the old dog dies there follows a grieving period not unlike that the Queen accorded Prince Albert. I've spent this autumn on long, solitary walks, tenderly remembering the years with my yellow dog. It has been a fruitful time of transition, what Colette called *fertiliser la douleur*, a fertilising sorrow.

But now I think we are ready for a puppy. This will be Sam's first dog of his own, and he wants a bitch. As this is not exactly puppy season, I've had to follow every lead. The telephone calls begin like this: 'Hello, this is Carla Carlisle at Wyken. I've been given your name because I'm looking for a labrador puppy. We're looking for a family dog (translate: £100) more than a gundog (read: £300+) although I will train her to the gun.'

The response, eight times out of nine, has been a pause, followed by: 'Didn't you get rid of the shoot at Wyken?' or 'I believe you're against shooting, is that right?'

It seems there is a fraternity out there who think that I am the pushy woman who doesn't believe in shooting. Here is the true story.

Once upon a time, I spent every Saturday morning with my boy cousins crossing fields and sitting silently in woods, in search of rabbits, squirrels and birds. The rules were simple: you kill it, you clean it, you eat it. We had to pay for our own cartridges with money we earned picking pecans, so we weren't exactly trigger happy.

I was not a natural shot but I was valuable because I had a good dog. Without a dog picking up, rough shooting is a frustrating business.

What I don't like is shooting driven pheasants. The set-up of beaters and guns. Reared birds (what I call yard birds). The ritual of the wife standing behind her man after the shooting lunch. The meals where the men all seem to be going deaf and everything the women say sounds stupid and banal because they have to say it so loud. You don't have to be a democrat with anarchist leanings to find the social life of a shooting weekend hard going.

We now have two shoots a year at Wyken, organised by and for local farmworkers. After lunch they swap round so that the guns are beaters for half the day. The money goes to a charity for sick children. When Sam is old enough, we will probably have a boys' shoot. I hope we will have it in October instead of the traditional January, because I think it's a mistake having boys' shoots when the days are cold and windy and the birds too testing.

One day I realised that I had lost interest in shooting. I sold my 4.10 and bought an electric Smith-Corona typewriter. They say girls grow up faster than boys. But I'm not opposed to shootin' and eatin' at all. I'm just a country woman determined to find a good dog.

November 14, 1996

PURE GIVING

THE kitchen table is covered with old copies of *Gourmet* magazine. It's a strange collection because it's nearly 20 years of Novembers, the worn covers featuring all the edible icons of Thanksgiving: pumpkin pie, golden brown turkey, cranberries in Waterford crystal bowls, sweet potato soup in pumpkin tureens.

These antique *Gourmets* are what's left after one of those heavy-hearted paring-down sessions. Like COUNTRY LIFE, *Gourmet* is a magazine that you do not easily part with. It was easier to ditch a couple of unpublished and unpublishable novels than my stacks of *Gourmet*. Finally, I decided I would keep just the November issues because when you live in England Thanksgiving is what you miss most about America.

And no, it is not like harvest festival. It goes much deeper than that. The third Thursday in November is the one day in the year when all Americans – Republicans, Democrats, men, women, rich, poor, black, white – do the same thing at the same time. Thanksgiving dinner is the single most American thing we have.

In the past, the liturgy of Thanksgiving was the celebration of plenty: a turkey so big it took a man to lift it out of the oven, sweet potatoes with melted marshmallows on top, fields of vegetables and acres of pumpkin and pecan desserts. We were especially thankful that we had more food and more choice than the Russians. Thanks to the Pilgrims, God was on our side.

I have to confess that I don't know if the Choctaw Indians I grew up with – now called native Americans – celebrated the way we did. Their version of that first harvest was probably rather different. For a start, the Indians did all the planting and harvesting. Then there were the small-pox-infected blankets we gave them, but we didn't hear about those until the late 1960s.

Even now my feelings about Thanksgiving keep changing. Today it is less about the celebration of plenty (Dear God, forgive us for what we are about to take for granted) and more a celebration of family. Family is what we all hunger for, and family is the scarcity we see all around us. But if thanks for that first harvest is what the original celebration was about, I find the second half of the word – giving – now occupies my thoughts.

The best true story I know about giving is told by the writer Anne Lamott in her book *Bird by Bird*. A little girl was dying of leukemia and her parents told her eight-year-old brother that she badly needed a blood transfusion. They explained that his blood was the same as hers and asked him if he could give his sister a pint of his blood, that it might be her only chance of living. He asked if he could think about it overnight.

The next day he told his parents that he wanted to give his sister his blood. At the hospital he lay on a bed next to his six-year-old sister and they were both hooked up to IVs. After a pint had been taken, the boy silently watched his blood dripping into his sister After a while the doctor came in and asked how he was doing. The little boy looked up and softly asked, 'How soon until I start to die?'

Somewhere along the way we have lost that innocence of pure giving. We've blunted our consciences with the belief that if we do not give, the state or the lottery will provide. It is the pilgrim inside us that needs nourishing, needs reminding that it is only in innocent giving that we show our true thankfulness.

Meanwhile, this Thanksgiving my menu includes free-range turkey pan-smoked over grape vines, cornbread dressing and giblet gravy, baked acorn squash, parsnip and celeriac puree, cranberry chutney and pecan pie with nuts from my family's trees. In other words, what we all want most of the time: traditional and amazing.

November 28, 1996

HOME ALONE

WE are walking down the Fulham Road, Alice and I, arm in arm, like a mother and daughter who enjoy one another's company. In fact, she is a few years older than my mother who died last year, but Alice seems like a contemporary.

Alice has been on a spree. She has bought earrings, a necklace, pearls and a tiara. Alice has always loved things that sparkle but this is her first visit to Butler & Wilson. Until now she has preferred the real, the old and the colourful: 17th – and 18th – century over 20th; emeralds and aquamarines (the colour of her eyes) over diamonds.

'You can't have everything,' she once told me. 'In my thirties I chose jewellery over analysis because it seemed a safer bet. My mother always said to keep one good piece up your sleeve that you can trade in for a facelift later on, and I did that too.'

Alice's husband loved buying his wife jewels. What man wouldn't – she has a long, slender neck and hands that were made for rings, long fingers with no brown spots and no bumpy knuckles. She has always gardened in gloves, her mother's creamy kid opera gloves because 'they really fit and you can still feel the roots'. We are in London today because Alice was burgled again last week. They didn't make off with the emeralds, 'just two rather good satinwood tables and a clock'. But Alice is feeling spooked now. She was lucky she wasn't there – she's lived on her own in her Queen Anne house in Lincolnshire since her husband died ten years ago – but a new and disturbing note has entered country-house burglary: 'They come when they know you are there, especially if you are on your own. Early in the evening when no alarms are on. They threaten you until you hand over the key to the safe.'

Today's shopping is entirely for bijoux for the safe. For years now Alice has been keeping her best jewellery in the refrigerator, under pillows in guest bedrooms, in video boxes. Her South Sea pearls nestle in a velvet pouch in *The Jewel in the Crown*. I once found a beautiful, old Cartier watch in wellies I'd borrowed to walk round her garden.

'Thank God for that,' she said, 'I promised to leave it to my hairdresser.' Alice's security system is not foolproof.

Alice believes that insuring jewellery, pictures and porcelain only provides 'the gangs' with their treasure maps. Although not inclined towards conspiracy theories, she is now convinced that the really thorough jobs done on the houses of her friends show a knowledge of the contents of the houses that only the insurers have. She stopped insuring 15 years ago. 'I spend September in Nantucket with a very old beau each year and I fly to Boston first-class on my Sun Alliance money – the money I would be paying out if I did insure.'

She does insure the house. 'It's been in this family for 400 years and if it burned down I'd like to think that my son could stick something up in its place.'

Now her plan is to put the Butler & Wilson jewels in the old S. J. Phillips boxes and install them in the safe. That way the burglars go off satisfied and are down the road 'before they realise that the batty old woman just had fakes'.

I admire her guts and her cheerfulness. She is as brave as she is elegant, but she no longer feels peaceful in the house she has lived in for more than 50 years. 'Everything has changed so much, but you can't go on moaning – lamentation is like the reverse of a face-lift.'

We decide to have a glass of champagne ('tea is so bad for your teeth') at Bibendum before I head back to Liverpool Street Station and home. We try on the loot and laugh at the *pièce de théâtre* that it represents. Alice is one of the sanest and funniest women I know. The problem is, Home Alone in the country is no joke.

December 5, 1996

STUFF AND JOY

SAM wants to know: are we rich or poor? I've spent so much of this child's life telling him that things cost too much, to take care of his bicycle, Doc Martens, cricket bat, because they cost a lot of money, and that coats have to last two years, that he isn't sure where we stand.

When I used to ask my mother which we were, rich or poor, she refused to tell me. I knew we weren't as poor as the black people who lived on the edges of our town and on our farm, and I knew we weren't as poor as Meg, Jo, Beth and Amy in *Little Women*. But I also knew that my grandfather managed the cotton plantation that he had once owned back in the Thirties, and that my parents worried (and argued) about bills each month.

But I want to give Sam an answer. For one thing, I think he needs to know how lucky he is. Lucky because he lives on a beautiful farm in one of the richest, safest, most honourable countries in the world. Lucky because he lives in a big house whose foundations have stood in the chalky earth for more than 400 years. Lucky because he is loved, healthy and strong. I want him to know that, yes, he is rich beyond the dreams of most people in this world. And I want him to know that we are not rich. That just because his friends have portable CD players and computers in their rooms, he can't. That shirts and shoes with Nike and Adidas written across them are no better than shirts and shoes with M&S written inside. And in case you think that I'm a truly wonderful person, perhaps I should confess that the first word Sam could read was GAP – emblazoned on his fleecy pullovers.

But now Sam is writing an important letter and he needs some answers. *Dear Father Christmas. How are you? I hope you aren't too tired. I've tried to be good this year.* What does he know? Does he suspect that Father Christmas doesn't have infinite resources after all?

From the beginning we explained St Nicholas's limits: he brings only three things and he never brings weapons. In those early years Sam wanted only one thing: at three, a red Massey Ferguson combine harvester; at four, a tent; at five, a castle. I bragged about the modesty of his requests, I glowed in my spiritual superiority to all the haggard mothers in Hamleys and Peter Jones.

And then I took up where Father Christmas left off, adding a herd of cows, sheep, pigs and a wooden farm to the red combine; a sleeping-bag and walkie talkies to the tent; lead soldiers, cannons and ramparts to the castle; a mountain of clothes, books and games. Dear God, please give my son the heart of St Francis of Assisi although his mother has the soul of Ivana Trump.

As I wander through the loaded shops, I want to have everything, to give everything. St Access of Visa is more flexible than St Nicholas. And then I remember the best Christmas I ever had. Under the tree was a pair of cowboy boots I had yearned for for what felt like all my life. In my stocking were oranges, Hershey kisses, marbles, two suspiciously familiar Indian arrowheads and a magical wart-remover.

More than anything I want to give Sam imagination and memory. To teach him that lots of stuff doesn't bring lots of happiness. I think it's probably all right that he knows the contents of the Toys 'R' Us catalogue by heart – when I was his age I could have passed an exam on the Sears and Roebuck Christmas catalogue. He will learn soon enough that those toys won't last.

What he really wants this year is a pair of goals so that he can transform the croquet lawn into a football pitch. I want to tell him that we aren't rich but we can afford that. Meanwhile, as I search for answers he goes on writing: *I have enough clothes and enough books. I would like a pair of goalkeeper's gloves.*

December 12, 1996

TRADITIONS

A FRIEND who lives in the next door village has just come back from a wedding in New Orleans. He's brought me the menu so that I can see the wines they drank with the ten-course dinner: '45 Comte Georges de Vogue Musigny, '66 Château Margaux, '75 Château Pétrus, '61 Romanée Conti La Tache, '85 Krug Champagne, '76 Château d'Yquem. While I gaze at the list, he tells me about the pre-nuptial agreement: if the marriage doesn't last a year, the bride will get only a million dollars.

My own prenuptial agreement was rather simpler. Before saying 'I will', I said I wouldn't. Wouldn't be tied to his family tradition of the Christmas rota: one year his whole family at Wyken, the next year at his sister's house in Warwickshire, then back at Wyken. Although Farrar & Co. were not called in to draw up the agreement, a promise was made.

But as surely as the star shone brightly in the East, so came the Wyken family Christmas. By then I had persuaded my husband that presents should be opened all together round the tree, with eggnog and coffee cake. That church would be followed by wild Irish smoked salmon and golden Gewurztraminer and then the Long Walk. Finally, at four o'clock, Christmas dinner is served, and the cook (who writes this) is relaxed and happy, and dinner is long and joyous.

I remember that first menu: *foie gras de canard frais*, followed by turkey with cornbread dressing, sweet potatoes with their sugary crust and, for dessert, Jane Grigson's frozen lemon souffle.

The menu we did not have was the one they all hankered after: charred chipolatas, dead Brussels sprouts, bread sauce that looks like a poultice, and, the Mickey Finn of all desserts, Christmas pudding. We were all tactful; we were all filled with secret longings.

But time changes everything, even how we celebrate Christmas. A few years ago, my mother-in-law, whom I had grown to love, died one early December. I relished that Christmas in Warwickshire where her three daughters and son began the painful task of being a family without her. And last year my own mother died. I no longer dream of going 'home' for Christmas.

Now our traditions are the ones that we create. My favourite is going to get our Christmas tree from our stand of wayward conifers. My husband goes out early and decorates a small tree with weighted candle holders and candles. At noon we head off with saw and axe, thermos of hot chocolate, and begin our journey. Just before we reach the tree, I distract Sam while his father runs ahead and lights the candles. Hand in hand, we come upon a magical, candlelit tree in the woods.

The glow on Sam's face for the first three years was my best Christmas present. This year he wants to help light the tree. He secretly brings along his red Sony cassette-player and as we come upon our magic tree Joan Baez is singing *Ave Maria*. Now Sam's great joy is the look on our faces.

On Boxing Day my husband and I have a ritual that is perfectly neutral: not English or Mississippi, but Wyken and our own. While everyone is still sleeping, we put on layers of clothes, hats and gloves. Armed with red Felco secateurs we walk to the vineyard where the vines march away in rows like a faded photograph of a First World War battlefield.

Such a dull and cold day seems an unpromising time to begin anything to do with growing, yet pruning is the single most important thing a grape grower does in a vineyard. The cuts we make in the bare, brown canes will determine more than anything else how much crop and of what quality will grow and, God willing, become wine on some warm afternoon next autumn.

Pruning, like Christmas, is an act of faith. I say a silent prayer and begin.

December 19/26, 1996

AULD LANG SYNE

FROM the time I was 12 until I was 16, I was in hot demand as a babysitter on New Year's Eve. After I got the children to bed, completed my inventory of the refrigerator, tried on the jewellery and shoes of the children's mother, and studied their wedding albums, I began the long vigil in black-and-white that would climax with everybody kissing in Times Square. It was the only night of the year that our television stations didn't sign off on the dot of midnight but lingered on, buzzing and hooting and singing *Auld Lang Syne*, although no American has any idea what those words mean.

Grateful parents paid me $20 for the night. In those days, before anyone had made the connection between danger and drinking and driving, I would be driven home in a car so thick with vapours of bourbon that the following morning I usually felt as though I had spent the night toasting with pink champagne.

I reckon those nights spent alone surrounded by

sleeping children marked me for life. Even now I don't hanker after singing and dancing and hugging and kissing on New Year's Eve. What I want is quiet. I need to edge gently into something as big as a new year.

An unexpected bonus of married life is getting to spend New Year's Eve at home. We dress in clothes our parents might have worn for dinner, light all the candles in the dining room, and have a feast as delicious as I can pull off. We drink a bottle of wine from the rack in the cellar which still bears the label written in my husband's father's hand after the Second World War: 'Rare and irreplaceable'.

This year we have promised Sam that he can stay up until midnight. He will probably manage the vigil with ease and delight. His parents will both be longing to read from their stack of Christmas books but will nobly play 'Outrage: Steal the Crown Jewels' instead.

I don't think I'm alone in preferring a subdued beginning to the new year. What astonishes the bank manager and our loyal clientele at our vineyard restaurant is that we have such a prolonged quiet spell: we close after lunch on Christmas Eve and do not open again until the second week in February.

In the beginning we shut because we figured nobody would want to come to bleakest Suffolk in January. Now that we are full all summer and winter, we shut because we all want a nice, long break. Christmas is our busiest season, and afterwards everyone needs time to relax, travel if they want to, or just paint the kitchen or train the new dog. In the vineyard the name for this phase of dormancy and renewal is quiescence. The vines are dormant now but this is when they will begin to store up the carbohydrates that will push out their buds when the temperature rises. You don't have to be David Attenborough to suspect that maybe folks have something in common with vines.

In a few days my father and I will kiss each other goodbye at Gatwick. I will say tearfully, 'I'm sorry we didn't have more time just to sit and talk.' He will say, 'Slow down, girl, just slow down.'

But meanwhile, on New Year's Day I will wake up with that wonderful feeling that I have a brand new chance to get it right. I will fill in those tiny spaces in my new diary, settling for Week-at-a-Glance although what I really want is Life-at-a-Glance. In another notebook I will write my familiar list of resolutions: get up earlier; drink eight glasses of water a day; do more exercise; spend less; answer all letters within a week; get organised. At lunch we will eat black-eyed peas for luck. I feel good about the days ahead. I too am an optimist's daughter.

January 2, 1997

MEDICAL TENDENCY

WHENEVER I come across a piece in the newspaper about a man who has been practising medicine in some Midlands town for ten years without so much as a biology A level, my heart goes to my feet. There but for the grace of God. You see, I am a quack, an incorrigible, medical quack.

Got a painful sore throat? Drink cups of very hot water. Catching a cold? Take three Isatis Gold tablets every two hours, a Chinese remedy I buy in bulk in Soho every autumn. At the hint of a symptom I diagnose and prescribe for everyone and their families on the Wyken payroll. I treat fevers, headaches, shingles, hayfever and burns. I even have a go at marital troubles and despair.

Mine is not merely a local practice. If a child falls on the escalator at Debenhams, I'm on the scene with my vial of Rescue Remedy and arnica administering to the hysterical child and reassuring the fraught mother. Was I aghast when the Princess of Wales was photographed in her green surgical mask? I was not. This is not a woman

120

who yearns for a slinky Armani pantsuit and Miriam Haskell pearls: my secret desire is for the little white coat and a stethoscope dangling casually round the neck.

So far I have managed to confine my medical tendencies to the safe side of the law. Just. Until I saw a mother slapping her small daughter in Marks & Spencer. The louder the little girl cried, the harder the mother hit. Almost dizzy with horror, I forced myself up to the woman. 'I'm a doctor,' I said quietly. 'If you hit your child again I will report you.' The shocked woman stopped and stared at me.

Only after she had left did I wonder: to whom would I report this woman? Perhaps more worrying, I felt no remorse for my fraudulent authority.

Which is not to say I'm not a conscientious quack. When *The Times* arrives each morning I scarcely glance at the front page, barely scan William Rees-Mogg, before settling down to study Dr Thomas Stuttaford's Medical Briefing. I keep my surgical scissors nearby, excellent for clipping out the articles that call for critical care ('The habit which kills one woman every 12 minutes') which go into my medical records.

When I am out of my medical depths, I make appointments for my patients at the local surgery. If I suspect that the care and attention provided is inadequate I am on the telephone pronto. The only time you will ever hear the words 'This is Lady Carlisle' uttered from my lips is when I am trying to penetrate the phalanx of receptionists at a medical facility. When my husband hears my diagnostic tones, he practices the art of being invisible. He thinks a little medical knowledge, combined with southern feudalism, is a dangerous thing.

But the truth is, in the heart of the countryside the NHS is a two-tier system. Not between the rich and the poor, but between the confident and articulate and the shy and bewildered. When a diagnosis is serious, I volunteer to go along to the appointment with the consultant. I write down a list of questions beforehand, and I make sure we get real answers. I take notes that we can study together when we get back home.

I suspect that the surgeries here in the country could do with fewer secretaries, receptionists, accountants. What they need is a patient's ombudsman, someone who would represent the patient, be reached on the telephone all day long, sit in on appointments if wanted and translate afterwards when needed. A patient's friend.

I realise that if these ombudsmen become established, it could mean the end of my part-time medical career. On the other hand, it would give me much-needed time to catch up with Dr Stuttaford, watch my videos of 999 and refine my wart-remover potions.

January 9, 1997

100 YEARS OF *COUNTRY LIFE*

I have loved England, dearly
and deeply,
Since that first morning, shining
and pure,
The white cliffs of Dover I saw
rising steeply
Out of the sea that once made
her secure.

So begins *The White Cliffs*, the epic poem that brought me minor fame in my small Mississippi town when I recited it, age 13, to the Kiwanis Club and the Chamber of Commerce. Looking back, the southern businessmen were an odd audience for a poem whose main purpose had been to bring America into the war by reminding her that, despite England's insularity, conceit, stodginess and social inequalities, she was fighting their war.

I still remember great hunks of the poem about the

American girl who falls in love with an Englishman. She goes with him to the family home in Devon, a manor house with gardens trampled by Cromwell's army, orchards of apples and pears, casements that had looked for the Armada.

> 'Of course you understand,'
>   he said, 'my brother
> Will have the place.' He smiled;
>   he was so sure
> The world was better
>   for primogeniture.
> And yet he loved that place,
>   as Englishmen
> Do love their native countryside,
>   and when
> This was home no more to him
> His life would shrink and
>   lose its meaning...'

It was many years later, after I had fallen in love with an Englishman, that I was truly able to conjure up that Devon house: rooms called scullery and larder, halls that were called passages and another room called the hall. And, unmentioned in the poem, the stacks of COUNTRY LIFE, copies kept for ever, progressing from the oak table in the hall to the walnut tables in the drawing room, before entering their final resting place in the guest rooms.

On a grey wintery day, England and poetry and COUNTRY LIFE all converge. Thanks to primogeniture, I now live in a Suffolk manor house, wife of an Englishman, and mother to a son and heir. I never think about the imminence of war. The ghost on the stairs nowadays is not war but an invasion never meant: Happy Eaters, BP stations and Travel Inns. The words that now echo in my heart are Philip Larkin's in *Going going*.

I thought it would last my time
That sense that, beyond the town,
There would always be fields and farm.

It seems, just now,
To be happening so very fast;
Despite all the land left free
    for the first time I feel somehow
That it isn't going to last...

And that will be England gone,
The shadows, the meadows, the lanes,
The guildhalls, the carved choirs.
There'll be books, it will linger on
In galleries; but all that remains
For us will be concrete and tyres.

Happy Birthday, COUNTRY LIFE. Long live country life.

January 16, 1997

THE PONTIAC PRINCIPLE

ALTHOUGH Mr Ballard always admired the smooth lines and suspension systems of Buicks, he drove Pontiacs all his life. The reason for this, he told his son, was that Mr DeLoach who had the Pontiac dealership in town, bought all his clothes, including his Sunday suits, from Ballard's department store. 'It's the civilised principle of free enterprise,' Mr Ballard explained.

Over the years, this concept has become known in my family as the 'Pontiac Principle'. My passionate adherence to this belief has caused my husband some awful moments. Like when in three meetings in a row, with the bank manager, our accountants and our local solicitors, I confessed that it was getting hard for us to hold on to our loyalties since the other bank in Bury St Edmunds, the other firm of accountants and the other solicitors were such good clients at our vineyard restaurant and country store. This wasn't strictly true, but true enough, and it sharpened some minds. Now Mr Boyden, our manager at

126

Barclays Bank, eats in the restaurant about once a month.

As we go deeper into the new year, I find myself chewing over the Pontiac Principle a lot of the time. Reluctant as I am to begin the risky process of finding a new hairdresser (I go only three times a year), I confess I'm getting tired of looking at myself in the mirror and smiling weakly while Viv says: 'I really must get out to your place one of these days.' Although I think Mr Rolfe is the most congenial and learned butcher in East Anglia, it's getting on my nerves that he has never eaten in the restaurant he supplies.

Don't get the wrong idea. The Pontiac Principle is alive in the countryside. Trevor Pollard, our builder, entertains his clients in the restaurant on a regular basis. He knows it's good for business for these folks to sit in the 400-year-old barn converted by his own expert craftsmen. Jane Capon delivers her unpasteurised organically produced Jersey cream to the restaurant kitchen and then goes shopping in the country store. Charles Morris, the Norfolk architect who is transforming our 1950s farm office into a modest Gothic Folly, holds office parties and family birthdays here. It seems to me that this is what economic unity is all about.

That's what's at the back of my thinking when I order stuff for our country store. Since the day I opened I've been trying to wage my own one-woman boycott against the Pacific Basin – more specifically, China. Even though it is hard work to find a Pooh Bear that isn't made in China (80% are, and even Paddington Bear is made in Indonesia), I do my utmost. I stock wellies made in Scotland and rugs made in Wales. I have pottery from Ireland, the last wheelbarrows made in England and bicycles made in Oxfordshire. The way I figure it, nobody from China ever comes to my shop and the Japanese aren't interested in importing Wyken wine, and therefore I don't feel obliged to contribute to their runaway trade surpluses.

I reckon that if more people understood and practiced the fundamental common sense of free enterprise, we wouldn't be losing all our village shops. Mr Fordham at Ixworth would still be operating his petrol pumps (and none of that self-service stuff, either) if everybody hadn't started filling up at the new Tesco. The truth is, we pay a great deal for the money we save.

My husband gets worried when I get to buckin' and snortin' but this time I'm going about it in the nicest possible way. As soon as the snow clears I'm going to deliver a few bottles of Wyken Bacchus with little notes attached. I'll be driving round the countryside in my Volvo from Cecil and Larter. But I have to tell you, if Mr Cecil and Mr Larter don't show up by Easter, I've got my eyes on a brand new Pontiac.

January 23, 1997

FAMILY MATTERS

SAM has a new friend whose father farms in Wattisfield, a few miles down the road. I can tell that he is now looking at his own family through new eyes. At first, the reappraisals were gentle. 'How come we never have proper Sunday lunch?' he asked as we sat down to scallops served on a bed of endives.

'What do you call this?'

'I mean English food. Beef, normal vegetables, Yorkshire pudding.'

I let it pass.

Then our inadequacies became more substantial. Not only does Fred Barker's father have a quad, one of those open-topped four-wheel vehicles that look like a cross between a golf cart and a tractor, he also drives a Shogun.

'We should get a Shogun, Papa. We could trade in the old Montego.'

My husband is not one of those farmers who is into kit.

I don't think he knows what a Shogun is because I hear Sam explain that it's like a Land Rover Discovery.

Then it comes out that the Barkers' tractors are all Case Internationals. I'm a John Deere woman myself. Over the years, I've slowly replaced all our Ford tractors with a fleet of the bright green machines. 'Nothing Runs Like a Deere,' I remind Sam, but he hasn't found that funny since he was six. 'We could have a Case on trial, just to try it out.' I explain how it's better to stick to one make and one dealer because that way you are considered a good customer and you get better service. The loyalty card doesn't impress him.

I'm trying to be extremely gentle with myself and take my new shortcomings in my stride. I still remember when I first realised that my parents weren't perfect. It, too, began with a new friend. Faye's father was a Methodist preacher who wasn't very nice to me, but it was his wife I adored. She was so sweet. She never yelled at her children, she wore blouses with Peter Pan collars, 'natural' lipstick and clear nail polish. She baked cakes from scratch when it was nobody's birthday. She smelled of Jergen's lotion.

My mother wore Persian blue eye shadow and black Capri pants. She had short hair, read poetry, smelled of Jungle Gardenia and smoked Pall Malls. She thought my friend's mother was 'pitiful' and her father was a bully.

Still, I had counted on Sam's uncritical love for a little longer. I've loved the way his face lights up when he sees me arrive to pick him up after school, like he's Tom Hanks and I'm Meg Ryan and the coat pegs are the top of the Empire State Building. Was I wrong to think that a country childhood would slow down the dawn of judgment? Are there no surprises in life? Anyway he's pretty lucky: I don't lock him outside to play during ice storms, even if he did tell Fred Barker that; and I make return trips to school when he's forgotten his swimming things/karate clothes/football shoes. Plus, I really like Fred's parents and I don't smoke Pall Malls.

I believe that it's best to brainwash your child as long as you can. I tell him that a mule is better than a quad anyway, and now that I'm a member of the British Mule Association we might have some luck finding one. That Shoguns are nice but in the end they are just four wheels and a motor. I tell him that I used to dream of having an aeroplane like all my farming cousins in the Delta, until one day I came across a line from Flannery O'Connor: 'I wouldn't give nothing for an aeroplane, even a buzzard can fly.'

I realise that winning back his approval is going to take some effort, so I'm having a go at roast beef and Yorkshire pudding this Sunday. To be on the safe side I'll be dressing like a Sunday School teacher. Meanwhile, the soundtrack for the school run this week is the best of B. B. King: 'Nobody loves you like your Mama and even she might be jiving.'

February 13, 1997

UPSHIFTING

WHEN my friend April went to university she changed her name to Ariel and never looked back. Now she works for a magazine in America with a circulation larger than the population of Wales, aimed at the babyboomers who are running the country. It seems that while these prosperous forty and fifty-somethings are sitting in offices masterminding the global economy, what they are really thinking about are Amish quilts draped over the back of rocking-chairs that sit on wraparound front porches overlooking the bluffs in Maine and Montana and Tennessee. Not so much COUNTRY LIFE as Country Lifestyle.

Still, I was surprised to get a telephone call from Ariel during supper last night.

'Sweetie, I've got this brilliant idea. We're doing a special issue on downshifting in the countryside and I want to do Wyken: the farm, the vineyard, the house, the yard, the restaurant, the chickens, the goats.'

'Sheep,' I say, 'we don't have goats.' I pause for a few more seconds. Something seems out of sync. Then I remember. 'Ariel, we aren't downshifting at Wyken. This is upshifting.'

A nervous laugh enters the kitchen straight from New York. 'Honey, over here it passes for downshifting. Chickens that sleep in the trees. A restaurant and country store you open part-time. Sweetie: you wear clogs and eat deer. You shear sheep. You are the Martha Stewart of downshifting.'

This troubles me. Not that I have anything against Martha Stewart. I bought a stack of her magazines at a garage sale in 1994 and they changed my life. I learned How to Iron a Shirt: collar first, then yoke, cuffs, sleeves, right front, back, left front (reverse last three steps if you're left-handed). Then I learned How to Make a Bed. That's a little more involved. I can send you a photocopy, but meanwhile, always start your hospital corners at the head.

So the problem isn't Martha Stewart. The problem is that downshifting, like cappuccino, Lycra and Harvey Nichols, is really an urban notion. The idea of simplifying your life, consciously deciding to earn less and spend less so that you can concentrate on the things that really matter, is not an option in the country. Everybody I know is living as simply as they can. There aren't a lot of hours to cut back on. Nobody can afford to cut back.

And yet, the 'quality of life' aspect of downshifting is a part of all my thinking. I was determined to create the 'humane' restaurant without the killer schedule of long hours and split shifts. I wanted to create ideal part-time employment, to put into practice my belief that everyone needs the security of a job, to feel a part of a community, and they need to have something of their very own. The vineyard manager and assistant have now planted their own two-acre vineyard in the walled garden at Ickworth, ten miles from here.

Lucy, our chef, genuinely downshifted when she left her job as head chef at London's Blue Print Cafe. Now she's ready to start her own cooking school at Wyken. Pippa, head waitress, is a textile designer with a greeting card business. Tony, our shop manager, designs tableware and styles for film shoots. I try to explain to Ariel that creative 'upshifting' is at the heart of the new rural development.

She doesn't even pause: 'Fabulous. I'll slot you in the issue on the New Utopias.'

P.S. Here's something else I learned from Martha Stewart. How to Cook Lobster: To keep the lobsters relaxed and tender, add half a cup of gin to the lukewarm water before plunging them in. Your lobsters will pass out long before the water reaches the boil. I know the feeling.

February 20, 1997

III
Growth

WARNINGS

At some hazy moment between ordering her eggs and bacon and reaching for her copy of *The Times*, my friend Valerie's Fendi handbag was stolen. The scene of the crime was the breakfast car on the train to Birmingham. Gone are her credit cards, passport, house keys, car keys, address book, reading glasses, Chanel lip gloss and favourite fountain pen.

'Consider yourself blessed,' I tell her.

Katie telephones from Wales. She has just ploughed her Vauxhall van into a roadside pillar-box while attempting to tune in Derek Cooper on *The Food Programme*. Her van will take two weeks to repair and she has to hire a car because she lives miles from anywhere.

'For this small accident you must be grateful,' I say.

I spend the morning making a *Silver Palate* carrot cake for the school bake sale and drive off with it on the roof of the car. In the frame of my rearview mirror, I watch the cake explode on the drive. Red-eyed in Tesco as I pay for the Wallace & Gromit substitute, I tell myself it was a close shave. A little blessing. Nobody got hurt.

At the heart of my thinking is my Minor Philosophy of Life, a belief that minor accidents and losses are our personal early warning system. These incidents are sent to tell us that through carelessness, sloth, overwork, insensitivity or lack of sleep, we are not concentrating; things are happening that don't have to happen. Recognising these irritating and depressing signals will help us find our bearings.

Although my solemn pronouncements do not endear me to my friends, I persevere. I tell them that loss of your handbag prevents you from walking, head down, into the path of that wayward Vauxhall van. A brush with a pillar-box spares you the head-on collision with the sugar-beet lorry.

My school of thought has nothing to do with the hocus pocus of seeing signs in the stars. And this way of thinking is no substitute for vital information. Valerie was informed that Fagin and his gang now wear Daks suits and operate the first-class carriages of British Rail trains only after she discovered her bag was gone. But she also knows that she wasn't concentrating.

When farmers are drowsy it is plain to see: fat hen takes over the sugar beet and CAP satellites register the crop as set-aside; the Walsham le Willows art class comes to paint the poppies in the field of barley. Yields go down.

When concentration flags in everyday life, the evidence is less obvious. Umbrellas, tickets for the dry cleaners, keys are lost. Friendships become fractured because you don't spend enough time together. These events are irksome but they aren't a disaster.

Friends urge me to lighten up but how can I? Even my cockerels crowing at dawn sound like sirens belting out calamity: New Day, New Danger. I see WARNING signs everywhere: BSE, *E. coli*, plummeting sperm counts. Maybe we are living in an age of warning overload. When the dire warning in the Marlboro man cigarette advertisement is bigger than the horse, it becomes a message you cannot heed.

Meanwhile, I think nervously about the man who has spent 30 years walking up and down Oxford Street wearing his sandwich-board warning about the dangers of protein. So far protein isn't on my list of worries. It's the vision of myself competing with him for space in front of Selfridges. My sign reads: 'Heed the Small Warnings in the Lost Keys. In the Dented Fender is Your Salvation'.

February 27, 1997

CAUSE AND EFFECT

THIS week the aconites and snowdrops came out together. This doesn't usually happen. According to custom, the intrepid little aconites come out first. The snowdrops procrastinate. The acid yellow aconites are like the warm-up musicians whose job is to stoke the frenzy before the big shots come on stage. Still, the sight of these brave little flowers in the cold sun fills me with relief, recalling lines I once saw on a poster in the Underground:

Oh, such a tidy world.
Seeing the April blossom my eyes water
Just for the sake of anything that works.

The poem was called *Walking Home* by Jonathan Aldrich, and for years I looked for it in bookshops. Apparently publishers were among the things that didn't work in the poet's life.

Here in the country it is possible to feel that most of the basic things in life still work. You drill the wheat and barley and it grows. You tend your crops by providing fertile soil and enough moisture, and you get healthy, high yields. Prune the vines with skill and care and you get ripe grapes that will become good wine. Cause and effect are visible, tangible, knowable and comforting. For better or for worse, we are generally more accepting in the countryside when things don't work. At Wyken the telephones frequently go dead. Our farm manager has the only mobile telephone, so when dial tones vanish, communication hits a certain lull. Because our line is a business line (the farm), British Telecom is supposed to respond right away but here on the prairies of Suffolk, BT is fairly relaxed. First they try to wriggle out of coming by accusing us of having 'equipment not owned by BT', but we've long since surrendered the Buzz Lightyear telephone to Sam's London cousins.

Surges in our electrical supply are even more common. They are also more familiar to me. In the late fifties, my Uncle Ham persuaded my grandmother to let him build some chicken houses on her farm. From the day the first thousand chicks arrived, lights in our own house dimmed and flickered like cheap candlelight. Our water supply dropped to a tepid trickle and for six months we bathed in two inches of water. In the end the chickens smothered each other during a tornado. My grandmother said it was the will of God and we went back to having baths deep enough to float the Ivory soap.

Power surges at Wyken were once confined to stints when the irrigation was running. Now they seem to occur any old time, jolting computers, clock radios and fax machines. When the power fails completely, we light candles, listen to the Roberts radio, and, after ten or 12 hours, crank up the generator bought by my husband's father in the Seventies during the three-day weeks. At the same time he bought a touchingly optimistic 'lifetime's supply' of whisky from the Wine Society. His heirs are grateful for both these prophetic investments.

Good-natured as we are about the little disturbances of country life, few of us feel cheerful about the vaster arenas of cause and effect. At the Suffolk Agricultural Association's spring conference last week in Ipswich, a climate specialist told us that in the next 50 years East Anglia is likely to see an all-round increase in temperature of two degrees and a 5% decrease in summer rainfall.

My fellow farmers thought I would feel pretty smug as the professor predicted that England's bread basket could turn into Europe's wine cellar. The truth is I think that global warming is scary and farmers haven't begun to understand. As much as I like to prance about claiming we are the new Medoc, we could just as easily be the new Oklahoma. Then truly will our eyes water just for the sake of anything that's green.

March 6, 1997

HICK MEMORIES

ONE of the nicest things about being a farmer in Suffolk, as opposed to being a farmer in America, is that nobody thinks you are a hick. Suffolk farmers are reckoned to have as much dignity, knowledge and social respectability as doctors and lawyers, and a great deal more than politicians and car dealers. Between Norwich and Colchester the word redneck isn't on anybody's lips, and that absence of contempt is a good thing.

True, the English are prone to romanticise country life but they never get romantic about farming. I think that's a good thing, too. Folks often romanticise what they have first despised.

So I almost glow with the respectability that comes with my job. But this is where it gets tricky, becomes the kind of situation my Aunt Edna describes as 'hair in the butter'. You see, respectability eats into the time spent at your day job, and my day job is farming.

All week long I've been trying to work in the

143

vineyard, preparing for the tractor that's coming in next Monday to yank out six rows of vines. That's one whole acre, a seventh of the vineyard, of healthy vines in the prime of their life. The problem is that, through no fault of their own, they are in the wrong place at the wrong time. They are Chardonnay and Pinot Noir eight miles north of Bury St Edmunds.

I planted them against all advice. 'Zay veel brek your heart,' warned Gaston, but I wanted some 'noble grapes', *pour ajouter un peu de noblesse* to my vineyard. Late-ripening French respectability v early-ripening German hicks. Trouble is, these little aristocrats ripen only every three years, and the vineyard financier, my husband, says we can't keep them in the hope that global warming gets its act together.

Thinking too highly of yourself, or of your climatic ability, is rarely economic. Replacing the vines will cost about £3 a vine plus a wait of three years before the new babies begin to crop. To dilute the cost, I've made a deal with the Forever Green Nurseries who are buying my beautiful, gnarled, biblical stems for 90 pence each. My Chardonnay vines will be turned into 'everlasting' bonsai trees.

Cutting the vines so that they are aesthetically right for the buyers at Forever Green is labour-intensive. It is also critical to get the vines' roots pulled up and the ground prepared for the planting, and all this really needs to be ready by early April. It's just that I've been too busy galloping round being respectable and sitting in meetings.

Judging is about to start for the Country Landowners Association Farm Buildings Award scheme, and more than a year ago I agreed to be chairman of the judges for this part of England. I'm not really good chairman material because I tend to subscribe to the old Maoist line of fewer and better meetings, but I care about encouraging farmers to build and preserve good farm buildings.

Meanwhile, I've written abject apologies to Historic Houses Association, St John Ambulance, Rainbow Appeal, Gardeners' Royal Benevolent Society, the Red Cross, four terrible diseases and the Shelter for Blue Tic Hounds because, respectable as I am, I do not have time to sit on their committees. I've said yes to the Suffolk Crafts Society because I have a weakness for beautiful, useful things made by people I know.

But the truth is, sometimes I hanker after the good old days when I wasn't considered nearly so respectable. When there was an invisible line as cold as a river between the farmer and the chairman of committees. When my Aunt Edna described me as the kind of girl 'who'd throw a skunk in a church house'. Some days I'd like just to get on with my day job and enjoy being a hick.

March 13, 1997

LIVES. TREASURES. HISTORY.

It is 6:45 in the morning and I am leaning on my baggage trolley at carousel 5, Terminal 4, Heathrow. I am mesmerised by the monotonous movement of the treadmill. The thump-de-thump of suitcases erupting from their hole stopped ten minutes ago. What's left are the orphans, stray bags that no one has claimed, including one which is identical to my American Tourister pullman in a colour called Driftwood.

Twice I have dragged it off the moving belt but this twin has a First Class baggage label and a British Airways Gold Club Executive address card. That is not me. I am a World Traveller, a flattering euphemism for someone who buys the cheapest tickets available. Even my First Class taste in baggage is a fraud: I bought mine yesterday on sale at the mall, three hours before my sister drove me to the airport.

Irritable and glum, I begin a mental inventory of the contents of my missing bag. My mother's silver. Twelve

146

place settings: dinner forks, salad forks, soup spoons, teaspoons, two sizes of knives, and pieces that only southern brides put on their wedding lists: pickle forks, nut dishes and long, slender iced-tea spoons.

Carefully wrapped in ancient Irish linen pillow cases: a portrait of Sam aged six, standing on bales of hay, wearing my old Davy Crockett hat with a real raccoon tail. And another portrait, a woman in her twenties, thin, headstrong, blond. The younger daughter. Me.

Providing padding for the portraits: letters home. Hundreds of letters, postmarked California, Georgia, France, England. These dutiful letters are my only archives, the story of my life.

Archives of my parents are also in the bag: the diary my father kept during the summer of 1964. Copies of their FBI file that they acquired under the Freedom of Information Act. More unlikely candidates for an FBI file are hard to imagine but my parents were white southerners who got involved in the civil rights movement. While we were living under a siege of bomb threats and burning crosses, the FBI informed us that they 'couldn't do anything until the house was actually bombed'. Well, they sure could make reports. A hundred pages of them with great hunks blacked out. Like the man in *The Trial*, we will never even know what was our crime.

I am bringing all these things back to England because in a few weeks my father is coming to live at Wyken. My father, independent, bookish, gentle. A patient man who looked after my mother night and day the last five years of her life. My father, whom I took to the oncologist on Wednesday where we were told that his is one of those cancers that makes invisible inroads while you are going about your life happily thinking that everything is just fine. Or, as in my father's case, playing cut-throat Monopoly at Christmas with Sam; complaining of the Balkan temperatures of English country houses; simultaneously reading a life of Tennyson and the latest John Grisham. My father who tells the oncologist: 'I respect your medical training but hell, I've got shoes in my closet older than you are.' My Pa who reckons it is both pragmatic and liberating to trust his own judgment about the road ahead.

At the BA desk a kind man tells me that the Gold Card Executive may have taken my case by mistake. He gives me a customs form to fill in so that my bag can be delivered to me in Suffolk when and if they locate it. I reach in my pocket for a pen and find a note in my father's handwriting. *'Old men must die, or the world would grow mouldy, would only breed the past again.* Comfort from Tennyson.' I know what my father would put on the customs form: Three Lives, Some Treasures, A History. But I am a weary World Traveller. I write: books, papers, used cutlery.

March 20, 1997

148

SAVING THE FARM

WHEN I look back on it, those early years of my marriage were the happiest days of my life. And I should just leave it at that because I don't want to cause my husband any sadness. But the truth is, I don't think I will ever again know such passionate, exciting, heady times, when every day unfolded like a blank canvas under a big, cloudless sky.

My giddiness did not come from the joy I felt at getting my man. No, my tickled gladness came from waking up every morning with Farm Diversification on my mind.

No cause ever thrilled me more than Facing the Future and Saving the Farm. I felt like Isak Dinesen with a happy ending. I was in love and on fire with ideas.

My earliest scheme was the llamas. Not your ordinary llama breeding programme but the Llama Jamas: Mama Llama Jama, Papa Llama Jama, Larry Llama Jama and Lulu Llama Jama. The whole world would clamour to visit the

149

Llama Jamas at Wyken, ecstatic families who had read all the books: The True Story of The Llama Jamas, The Llama Jamas in Paris, in London, in New York, and so on, travelling round the world in their stretch llamasine.

The books, the film and then the 100% cotton, velvety pyjamas (Llama Jamas, got it?) yearned for by every child in the Western world. I researched fire-retardant fabrics in textile mills in Stoke-on-Trent. I persuaded my husband we needed to take out international trademarks.

And when the response hit a certain lull, I moved on to buffalo. What I don't know about buffalo management and marketing hasn't been written. As I gazed out on the vast plains of Suffolk, I could see the great beasts bending into the Siberian winds. I visited Wray and Roma Dawson on their buffalo ranch in Virginia to see how to build the corrals – you can't drive buffalo, you can only lead them. I brought back a suitcase of buffalo steaks and preached about the meat of the future: low in cholesterol and fat, with more protein and flavour than beef. I served rare buffalo and gratin potatoes with Château Margaux to my in-laws on Boxing Day. I sang 'Oh give me a home, Where the buffalo roam' to my little baby instead of lullabies.

And then one hot summer day I went with my husband to examine a crop of sugar beet on our lightest field. While he studied the shrivelled crop, I looked at the land: sandy loam over chalk, on a south-facing slope so steep that a tractor would topple over. 'Vines!' I hollered. 'This is a vineyard!' The Romans had cottoned onto that same idea but it felt like eureka to me.

But committing yourself to a diversification project is like getting married. You have to quit looking over your shoulder. Be faithful. It's like going to the school dance: you have to stay with the one who brung ya.

Of course, I'm mighty proud of our wine and the vineyard restaurant. The whole Diversification Shoeshine. But I do miss the dreaming. Just the other day I thought of a plan that would carry us right into the Millennium, inspired by Dolly and that 14-year-old boy in New York who has cloned a frog. My company would be called Clone-a-Pet. Imagine how much happier the human race would be if we could clone our beloved hounds. 'A Dog is Not Just A Dog For Life.'

I was about to explain to my husband that the old stables could be converted into Clone-a-Pet plc headquarters when the trademark renewals for Llama Jamas in Brazil came through the post.

'Do you think we still need these?' he asked.

Like I said, those early days were the best. Before I realised that the reason the sky is so big is because there aren't any trees.

March 27, 1997

151

ALL PROPERTY IS THEFT

CALL me Princess Smartypants but I think I've got something to say to the vicar who thinks it is morally correct to steal from supermarkets. Because I have. Not on a regular basis. My crime was a one-off, *à l'improviste*, a tender, pale pink veal roast in a Felix Potin in the 14th Arrondisement in Paris back in the 1970s.

If my crime had been premeditated, I would have gone for a more discreet object of desire, such as the little bag of *morilles*, those rich mushrooms that look like dried prunes and cost twice as much as the joint of baby cow. But my accomplice was a hyperactive treadmill pushing my groceries faster than *madame* at the till could register, practically shoving the *rôti* (40FF) into my string shopping bag.

Browned lightly, roasted, and served with a sauce of Marsala, *crème fraîche* and *morilles*, the veal was succulent and satisfying. Adding to its flavour was my ignorance of its babyhood, and a fondness for the rallying cry of the 19th-century French anarchist Jean Proudhon: 'All

Property is Theft'. All in all, a conscience-free meal.

My success might well have inspired a career as a *gourmande* Holly Golightly, but only days later I witnessed a young Algerian being frog-marched through a Monoprix and shoved into a black Maria. It was like a scene from a Nazi movie and for years afterward I was haunted by replays of the image of the frightened man. French police are not tolerant, even of white-skinned foreigners. The thought of being shoved into a police van and deported for *porc aux pruneaux* seemed to me an ignoble fate.

But not once did 'Thou Shalt Not Steal' pop into my head. I was on the road of righteous indignation, convinced that the *supermarchés* appearing near every metro stop in Paris, would destroy the beautiful street markets which were the heart and soul of every *quartier*.

Now I've changed territory and my concerns are different. Or are they? My specialist subject on Mastermind could easily be 'Supermarket Comparisons'. In fewer than eight years my local market town Bury St Edmunds has acquired a new Sainsbury's, Waitrose and Tesco. Rumour has it Asda is on the way.

You don't have to be a sociologist to see what these food giants do to country life: jobs lost, the crowning of car power, life sucked out of villages, and the tyrannising of English farmers with talk of cheaper 'carrots from Poland' at every meeting.

Nor do I like being a collaborator, abandoning local shops in favour of easy parking, balsamic vinegar, rocket, limes and corn on the cob. My head may never be shaved in punishment for my complicity in the crime of flying food round the world in refrigerated aeroplanes, but I am guilty.

The difference now is that I would feel no better if I walked out with a plucked but unscanned guinea fowl. I see the futility of the gesture. Now I'd like just to force some community consciousness onto the food giants. I'd like planning laws to require all new supermarkets to include community rooms which could be hired cheaply and used for Italian classes, yoga groups, readings, first-aid workshops, a place to bring people together for something more than profit.

And those creepy coffee shops need to move with the times, become places where you might want to meet a friend. Why sell bagels and Italian coffee inside and offer only jam doughnuts and phoney cappuccinos in the coffee shop?

The truth is, the food giants are here to stay, but we don't have to be such suckers. Country citizens could insist that for every supermarket built, TescoSainsbury's & Company has to provide a cricket pitch or a bowling green in a neighbouring village. It wouldn't amount to more than a veal roast for the food giants, but it could mean the whole world for this endangered thing called the rural community.

April 3, 1997

154

SILK CUTS

I AM at a midday drinks party in an 18th-century folly on one of Suffolk's most perfect estates when one of the guests comes up to me.

'I had a great meal at your restaurant a few months ago. Wild salmon pan-smoked over vine prunings, your gold medal Bacchus. Delicious.'

I'm just about to shuffle my feet and say 'Aw, shucks' when he adds: 'Shame I won't be coming back again.'

Say what? Eggshells in the almond tart? Car sickness on the way home? He helps me out: 'I never knowingly go to restaurants that don't permit smoking. I consider smoking part of the pleasure of good food and wine. And I don't feel the need to subsidise dictators.'

'By golly you are right, and I'll drink to that,' I wish I had said. Instead, I got into a really stupid argument, defending my little smoke-free zone like it was the Gospels and I was a Baptist missionary.

An important critic comes to the restaurant and we all

pretend we don't know who she is. Between each course she goes out into the cool evening for a cigarette. When it starts to drizzle we offer her an umbrella from a stash we keep just for smoking friends. The nylon shield seems inadequate provision to this woman who, it must be said, is one of the most influential food writers in the country.

An elegant woman dressed in new Jaeger and old pearls takes a cigarette from a silver case that looks like a gift with an engraved inscription from Cole Porter. Charles, the sweetest headwaiter in the world, gently informs her that there is no smoking in the barn. Anxious not to hurt anyone's feelings, we've concocted a story about ancient wood buildings, fire risk and insurance rates. 'I'm surprised they let you have a stove', she replies sharply. We realise we must refine our story.

A no-smoking restaurant was fairly rare when we opened nearly five years ago. A few country restaurants were beginning to provide non-smoking areas, but in the cathedral-like space of the barn, there was no good way to divide it. Besides, I didn't want to. One little whiff of Benson & Hedges and I go right off my lemon posset.

And there is another problem. Smoking in restaurants seems such an urban thing. I got it into my head that a vineyard restaurant should smell of fresh food, newly mown hay, beeswax and old roses. But here comes the rub: city folk like to eat in country restaurants, and city folk – especially young city folk – love to smoke.

The most passionate smokers I know are young women and chefs. They are the Silk Cut syndicate. I pride myself on being able to cure just about anything from athlete's foot to xenophobia but the one thing I never make any headway with is smoking. I provide nicotine patches and pay for hypnosis. I rant the statistics: in parts of England more women are dying each year from lung cancer than breast cancer; five women smokers die every hour in this country from diseases caused by or exacerbated by their habit, nearly 43,000 each year. But these young women are like Mississippi crocodiles: they don't budge an inch.

I used to have this fantasy of a French lover, more Jean Gabin than Jean-Paul Belmondo. After we'd made love he would light up a Gauloise and I would lie in the crook of his arm (not a comfortable position as you know) and watch the thick smoke waft in the air. Another fantasy: that I would be a real writer, with a cigarette dangling from my lips and an ashtray full of cigarette butts next to my typewriter. I failed on both counts.

Still, I believe that the rights of people who want to eat and drink in a smoke-free setting have to outweigh the rights of real writers and French lovers. Country air may not be all that it is cracked up to be but it is the best air we've got. I'll drink to that.

April 10, 1997

THE BROOCH GARDEN

ON my 40th birthday my husband produced a diamond brooch from the cigar box that is kept locked up in the gun cupboard. It was one of those brooches that comes apart and you can clip the two pieces onto your dress. I think they are called diamond clips.

'Oh sweetheart,' I said, 'you shouldn't have.'

I waited a few tactful days before I asked: 'Can we sell these and create a garden in the front of the house?' One of the things that baffle people not to the manor born is the bleak, unwelcoming fronts of English country houses, all gravel and cars. We can't understand why the beauty and grandeur – the garden – is on the other side, in the backyard, so to speak.

So, instead of diamond clips we now have espaliered apples, a quincunx inspired by an early design by Gertrude Jekyll, rocking-chairs for watching sunsets. There's nary a car in sight.

When the pearl and diamond earrings from Richard

Ogden's were presented on a significant anniversary I whispered: 'These are beautiful.' It took me three days to confess that what I really hankered after was an avenue of limes that would connect the garden to the wood. The man at Richard Ogden's was a prince of understanding and the trees, *Tilia x euchlora*, are now 12ft tall.

Predictably, my husband has become a little discouraged. Many years may pass before I find a little Moroccan leather box with velvet lining nestled on the breakfast table. I say this with some sadness. Not because I yearn for jewels but because I have truly loved converting the sparkling heirlooms and other bijoux into big projects. Simply to agree on a project as a present seems to lack punctuation.

Much nicer to think that the diamond watch, made for a wrist more slender than my own, might become a pond outside the rose garden; the pearl choker made for an ancestor's long neck become the thatched poet's house in the pond's centre. (Did Great-aunt Sophie know the pearls were real but the regal emerald clasp paste? Alas a pond but no poet's hut.)

The truth is, life, like farming, has its cycles. Although I still feel faithful to amber I bought in the Vienna flea market, the turquoise and amethyst necklace I got in Mexico, the earrings my mother gave me when Sam was christened, I've entered that time of life when indulging in ten *Verbascum* Helen Johnson means more to me than a pair of gold hoop earrings; the two wildly expensive standard wisteria now posted at the entrance to the herb garden excite me more than a double strand of lapis beads.

At the back of my mind is Gertrude Stein's belief that you can either collect paintings or buy clothes. For 40 years she dressed in a changeless blue serge uniform and bought paintings by Picasso and Cézanne. In my more modest (go on, write it:) middle age, I've gone for tree peonies and roses from Peter Beales. Although I still feel as girlish as I was when I didn't know my *Quercus* from my *Prunus*, I suspect there is an inverse connection between hormone levels and horticultural passion.

Or perhaps it is simply the desire to feel some control over a small patch of a chaotic universe. On an average day I feel that the big decisions in my life as farmer, wife and mother are made in Brussels, Westminster, Wall Street, City boardrooms. But when I walk through the dell and look at the 40 newly planted *Jacquemontii* birch, I feel that here, a mere acre from our farmland whose every crop is dictated from afar, I am queen for a day. By the time the brown bark of the adolescent trees turn their snowy white of middle age, I will positively glow in my jacket and skirt of indigo blue serge.

April 17, 1997

160

SMALL FATALITIES

DEATH is a way of life in the countryside. In order to get your stripes as a true countryman you need the heart of a Mafia boss. Better still, you need to have a trigger finger honed and perfected early in life. While city children were learning to read, you should have been learning to hit moving targets.

In fact, nothing upsets the balance of the farmer's peaceable kingdom like the written word. Too much Dick King-Smith and you'll never survive country life.

Every morning I feed the chickens and peacocks in the apple orchard. This is a satisfying way to start the day because they always look so pleased to see me. But no sooner am I back in the kitchen than a rat strolls out from his des res under the oil tank. Calm as you please, he tucks in to his *petit déjeuner* of kibbled corn.

Rats are as much a part of farm life as old tractor tyres and rusty ploughs. If you have a barn and a bale of hay you have rats. But rats give most people the creeps, and when you have a garden open to the public, you don't want rats that sun themselves in the apple orchard like they were house cats. This means you have to go into the cellar, get out the 12-bore, and walk slowly and silently to the breakfast scene. Just as the rat cocks his head as if to ask: 'What do you have to do to get a decaf cappuccino round here?' you fire.

Plonking the corpse into the green wheelie bin, you do not dwell on rodential literature. Unless you think about Templeton in *Charlotte's Web*, the rat that lives under pig Wilbur's trough. 'The rat had no morals, no conscience, no scruples, no consideration, no milk of rodent kindness no compunction, no higher feeling, no friendliness, no anything.' Templeton grudges help to others, then brags about it. He acts like a spoiled child. Problem is, literature fuzzes over everything. By the end of the book even the ratty Templeton becomes a rat you couldn't shoot.

The next creature on my hit list is the kestrel living in the eaves above an ancient limewashed wall. The coppery red that was once the original Suffolk pink, is now streaked with chalky white suggesting the influence of Jackson Pollock. So potent is this killer bird's paint matter that the encrusted security lights now dangle uselessly.

At dusk I go out with a bag of black-eyed peas and my pea shooter made from an old fax paper roll. When the peas are used up, I wave my arms and shout 'hee-haw' in a vain attempt to shoo him off. My husband thinks 'shoo' is just a southern euphemism for 'shoot'. He defends the protected kestrel's right to life because (a) he doesn't want me to go to gaol and (b) he insists that the kestrel's diet of frogs, house sparrows, lizards and field mice is quite harmless. I'm fatally fed up with sparrowhawks and kestrels who now have more rights than political refugees.

I confess my killer instincts sometimes wane. After watching *Babe*, bacon lost its appeal. Last week Sam and I wept as we watched *Fly Away Home*, about a kindly girl who saves a flock of Canada geese.

For 120 minutes I forgot about the damage these handsome aggressive vermin do to cereals, grasses and root crops. Last year we watched helplessly as they devoured 30% of a neighbour's wheat crop. But before my tears had dried, I reminded myself that the good Igor was touching only because he was 3,000 miles away. When he and his 15 garrulous siblings start hanging out in the oil-seed rape, they'll be lucky if all that comes their way is black-eyed peas.

April 24, 1997

DENTAL FLOSS

AT a dinner in London, the guest on my left begins: 'I've spent the past six weeks having a root canal and during this time I feel I've really got to know you.' Over coffee an elegant woman dressed in Jean Muir confides: 'My problem is my gums. Before I began seeing this Harley Street specialist, I was exposing bone round my second and third molars. But I do think you were heartless about the Grundys.'

These dental confessions awaken in me a throbbing nostalgia, like memory surfacing through a sea of novocaine, as I recall the deep armchairs in the oak-panelled waiting room in Devonshire Place. There I, too, once read fresh copies of COUNTRY LIFE: gambolling with otters, red squirrel and wandering dogs in Ian Niall's 'A Countryman's Notes', then studying Staffordshire enamels and Meissen teapots with Frank Davis in 'Talking About Salerooms.' Excursions into these dream worlds were a satisfying bonus of my investment in the delicate gold inlays that Mr McLean was putting in my teeth.

Now I go to Mrs Hassan's dental surgery in Hopton, two villages away. In the sunny little waiting room, I no longer track the comeback of otters, learn how to decipher the games that magpies play. Instead, I read that Roy Orbison's widow, Barbara, still feels her loss eight years after the singer's death. I study exclusive photographs of the sunset wedding in Hawaii of Capt. Mark Phillips and Sandy Pflueger. And I reflect: nowhere is there greater testimony to the efficacy of fluoride, orthodontia and Rembrandt dental bleach than in the pages of *Hello!*

Once upon a time, not long ago, people who lived in the country did not go to country dentists. The dentist was like the countryman's London club, its thick-carpeted waiting-room like the library where small talk is discouraged. If on a Friday evening you encountered a piece of shot in your roast pheasant, thus triggering a painfully exposed nerve, you stoically managed with whisky and clove oil until the journey up to London could be arranged. Even children qualified: our cousin Richard's sole memory of black taxis as a child are his trips up to London from Inkpen to visit the dentist.

But I suppose that soon these memories will become as dated and charming as descriptions of life in a novel by Evelyn Waugh. Now, however you get there, the journey to London is expensive and complicated. The London dentist, like the London tailor, the London solicitor, the

London accountant, has become a time-consuming luxury that only makes life in the country more complicated. The secret to the good life is to bite the bullet and find a good country dentist.

My dentist is the wife of the local doctor. Jo has three children and works part-time. She first saw me as an emergency patient three years ago and I've been going to her regularly ever since. We like the same writers and swap books back and forth. We try to meet for lunch every few months. I try not to stare at her white teeth.

Leaving your London dentist will not be easy. At first you will feel faithless. As you wait in the new surroundings you may have second thoughts. There will be the shock of hearing Radio 2 or Classic FM instead of the familiar funereal silence. And if *Hello!* and old copies of the *Sainsbury Magazine* don't appeal to you, I suggest that you bring your own reading material.

Once your feet are above your head and your mouth is open wide, you will find comfort in the state-of-the-art equipment. You will relish the conscientious endeavour to save every tooth and the honourable costings for porcelain crowns. You may not end up with a smile like that of Tiger Woods, but I guarantee you will have a sweet inner grin.

May 1, 1997

ROSE COUNTRY

MY friend Rose is wry, sardonic, modest, energetic and lean. When she discovered her husband was having an affair with the village fortune-teller/curtain maker, she enrolled in law school. Three years later, and three weeks after she qualified, Rose filed for divorce. She represented herself and emerged from the courtroom with the family home, a hefty one-off payment and a brand new Volvo stationwagon. Predictably, she now has a client list that reads like the Garden Club of America.

Once a year Rose comes to visit. At Wyken she gets up before I do, runs five miles, and has fresh-squeezed orange juice on the table when I come into the kitchen. She teaches Sam how to pass an American football and explains to him the principles of the Hay diet.

Over a breakfast in which protein and carbohydrate do not intermarry, Rose threatens never to speak to me again if I allow Sam to go to boarding school in September. When I shyly remind her that her son, my godson, is in his first year at St Paul's in New Hampshire, and loving it, she points out that he was 15 before he got shipped off to the American version of Eton.

According to Rose, a child belongs at home until he can beat his parents at tennis and reads Walt Whitman and John Updike for pleasure. I hem and haw about the merits of weekly boarding but this just makes her snappish. Rose does not believe that love conquers all, that good outweighs evil, that at the 11th hour something gloriously triumphant will prevent the worst before it happens. So free from all mystic expectation is Rose that I feel dopey eating my toast and blackberry jam in my T-shirt with the words 'Just Do It' emblazoned across my chest. Rose wears no message on her faded pink Brooks Brothers polo shirt: she just does it.

Over the years I've slowly bequeathed to Rose all the size six and eight clothes that fill my pre-country-life museum. A couple of visits back I swapped my velvet Chanel jacket for her Orvis suitcase on wheels. The jacket was a couture treasure I'd acquired from Pandora's in the good old days when it was located off Sloane Square. Sadly, this chic little creation seems to have shrunk while languishing in the cupboard. But much as Rose coveted the jacket, she tried to talk sense into me: 'The jacket is irreplaceable. You can order this suitcase from the Orvis catalogue whenever you like. Besides,' she said, 'just because you live in the country you mustn't let yourself go.'

Rose worries that the only underwear range I know is Marks & Spencer's. She worries that I'm becoming like those English women who cut their own hair in order to mend the roof. I don't dare confess that I trim mine already, not so much for roof repairs, but because I begrudge the car journey, the parking, the time spent.

But her concerns about life in the country are not merely physical. She sees moral pitfalls in the acres of cow parsley. She thinks that country life is bad for women, that it wears away a woman's natural optimism and before we know it, we are facing the vicissitudes of life with the rueful acceptance of survivors.

'Think of all those women who burned their bras in a gesture toward freedom. You country women ought to burn your driving licences. That would put you all on the road to liberation,' she opines on the 20-minute return journey of the morning school run.

In my heart I know there is a kernel of truth in her words. Still, burning anything seems as drastic as it is futile. Instead, I promise her I'll try the Hay diet, get a decent haircut and buy some Donna Karan silky sheer stockings. Maybe if I just do it, I'll be as tough and cheery and skinny as Rose.

May 15, 1997

BOOK MOURNING

MY idea of heaven is an empty house, a pot of strong coffee, cat and dog sleeping off their breakfast, and time to tuck into the obituaries.

Over the years I have established a routine. First I look for women. An anthropologist from Mars could easily conclude that on this planet men die more often than women, at least according to the obituaries of *The Times* and *The Telegraph*.

Next I check the ages of the deceased. I heave a sigh of relief when I see dates such as 1899 and 1902 and I take a deep breath when I see 1949, 1955, 1969. Although my natural inclination is to search for the cause of death, ever since I became the mother of an only child I look for those telegraphic lines that sum up years of married and family life so meagrely: 'wife Philippa and four sons' or 'marriage dissolved, one daughter'.

This is how I came across my old buddy Helene Hanff last week, her laughing, careworn, wrinkled face smiling at me as if to say: 'Still in your dressing-gown at ten in the morning? Good for you.' Although we never met, like most people who read *84 Charing Cross Road* I felt like I had a lot in common with this itinerant, rather Bohemian woman who had a passion for English literature.

'Few writers have sailed to fame in so slender a craft,' wrote *The Times*, referring to her 96-page lavishly spaced book containing the correspondence between the impecunious American writer and the London bookshop. It made me long to find my copy of that slender craft and spend a few minutes with my Anglophile compatriot who loved Hazlitt, Donne, Landor and Pepys, and who, in 1950, shipped 6lb hams and eggs in their shells across the Atlantic to the bookshop staff.

Alas, I did not spend a nice quarter of an hour dipping into my favourite bits. Dear Helene Hanff, who kindly led me to Walton's *Lives* and Lamb's *Essays of Elia* during a hot summer long ago, has vanished from my bookshelves as surely as she has vanished from this earth.

After my fretful search I began vaguely to remember loaning it to a book-loving friend a few years back. But who, who, who?

To console myself for my loss I decided to look for my 1848 edition of Walton's *Lives* which I lovingly purchased on a stall in Cambridge market on one of my first trips to England. On the shelf where it should have been, next to *The Compleat Angler*, was almost a space.

And then I remember its departure, a few Christmases ago, loaning it to a visiting scholar who, like Helene Hanff, was rivetted by the story of John Donne's elopement with the boss's daughter, landing up in the Tower for it, and nearly starving to death before getting religion.

Nothing is worse than mourning for books you have loaned out and will never see again. Of course some don't matter. I don't miss the *Cantos* of Ezra Pound and the truth is, I never could finish *Finnegan's Wake*. But I often think of my autobiography of Lincoln Steffens, my out-of-print Mavis Gallants. I pine for my original copy of *The Joy of Cooking*.

My own borrowing is not without blame. Once I wrote a cheque to my local library for £32 for Henry James's *The Golden Bowl* which was two years overdue and available at the time in Penguin paperback for £1.95. I still have Johnny Apple's *Paris Was Yesterday*.

But Helene Hanff captured perfectly the joy of owning books, the rich pleasure of the right edition, the favourite translation, blue leather bindings, marbled endpapers. In her honour I'm revisiting my shelves. And to whom it may concern: I'd like Sybille Bedford's *A Legacy* back now.

May 22, 1997

172

FRENCH OAK

I HAVE just written a cheque for an amount greater than my parents paid for their first home. It is also four times as much as I paid for any of my pre-marital cars. I could go further: what I am paying for 11 new French oak barrels would support a family of four for a year in most parts of the world.

Not that it was a case of either/or. Before I signed the cheque I wasn't thinking, should I go for the French oak or for the family in Albania? On the whole, I believe it is better to avoid these juxtapositions in life: should we eat at Bibendum or educate the children? Should we order the white asparagus or buy new tyres for the car?

But still, choices have to be made and battles fought. The farm manager is keen to replace our irrigation, a rare breed made in Romania and acquired some 15 years ago when the farm was managed by Bidwells. Lucy, our Chef in the vineyard restaurant, yearns for a new refrigerator and an ice cream machine. My husband wants a pond outside the rose garden. The barrels (now referred to around here as 'Carla's barrels') will put all these other desires on hold.

Until now, all our red wine has gone into two-year-old barrels from *grand crus* vineyards in France. Even hand-me-down barrels are not cheap because they are very heavy and take up a lot of space on the kind of lorries that I would like to see banned from the roads. But last year our red wine made a great leap forward and now has the flavour and authority that would benefit from new oak. I maintain that our reputation will finally rest on our Wyken Red wine.

Others do not agree with me. Naturally, Lucy believes that our reputation will stand or fall on the restaurant. My husband believes that the garden is the heart of Wyken. The farm manager believes it is the wheat, barley, rape and sugar beet that bankroll the whole shoeshine. The farm is like a big family in which everyone wants something different. The problem is, wanting something, and getting it, require a nerve-wracking mix of optimism and bossiness. My optimism was based on the 1,000 bottles we produced in 1995, stunning red wine that deserved new oak. The way wood influences the smell and taste of wine is complicated. In France alone there are five varieties of oak, the most prized from the Tronçais forest.

Winemakers talk about how the oak is seasoned. They debate the way the barrels are made (hand-split staves versus machine-sawn staves) and the level of toasting. I am scathing of colleagues who dump oak chips in their wines and think that will provide the 'kiss of oak'.

Two days ago we had a frost. Frost is a clear, capricious killer. Walking up and down the rows of red-wine grapes, I reckoned that 20% of the new shoots were hanging forlorn and mournful. Dead. Anxiety about investing in the French oak barrels grew worse with every vine. I had so nearly put that money on an old fire engine for sale in Norfolk, with the idea of installing a frost alarm in our bedroom. At $33°F$ the bell would ring and off I'd go to fill the hoses at our bore hole. It takes only one half-hour at $31°F$ to kill new growth, but water applied at a steady rate of $^{12}/_{100}$ of an inch per hour can keep the grapes alive. The artificial rain encases the vines in ice. But as my farm manager pointed out, the Romanian irrigation pump would probably break down while refilling the hoses, the ice could melt, the buds freeze, the crop would be lost.

Investing money and making wine is like making love. Once you think about it objectively, the romance is gone.

May 29, 1997

GOOSE BUMPS

MOST Sundays in winter I make pancakes for breakfast. A gallon of L. L. Bean maple syrup lasts us from November until April, when we move onto fruit salads, Greek yogurt and bran muffins.

But even though we've had pancake weather several Sundays lately, nothing has enticed us back to the griddle. Sam and I are embarked on a marathon of Kellogg's Sustain, the 'scientific balance of grains, fruits and nuts chosen by top sportsmen'. It is also the cereal that is offering five red Volkswagen convertibles for an 'instant win'.

Don't get the idea that I believe that if we eat enough of this fibre-stuffed cereal we might open a box with a winning voucher tucked inside. To tell the truth, I don't even expect to win one of the 5,000 Adidas T-shirts 'as worn by Tim Henman'. What I am celebrating with every bowl of the light flakes and juicy raisins is that Sam can now read the cereal box.

There are many celebrations in motherhood. The first toothless smile of recognition. The first night of uninterrupted sleep. The first real word ('tractor'). Memorable big moments in fatherhood seem to come later: the first win, age five, at sports day; signs of cricketing genius, age six.

But I'm happy because I watch my child gazing at the cereal box in the time-honoured tradition of needing to fix on the printed word at the beginning of the day. True, 'avantgarde' slowed him down, but he broke it into bits and mastered it. He rhymed 'Cabriolet' with violet, but I gently corrected him. He hopes we win as he knows I want an air-conditioned car, and he thinks a convertible is just that.

Mastering the cereal box is a triumph for Sam, too. Reading hasn't been an easy, seamless thing for him. Cool, shy, mystified, he watched as his friend, Kayleigh, two years younger, whipped through stories at age five that were still closed books to him at seven. I agonised, one minute being as patient as Mary Poppins, the next minute reducing him to tears with: 'But you knew that word yesterday.'

He's a country boy, I told myself. Before he was two, he would point to the vast arcs of water over the sugar beet and joyously say, 'ear-ra-gay-shun'. Before he could sing his alphabet he could distinguish wheat from barley, identify every make of tractor and farm equipment.

My friend Sheila, a primary head teacher in London, pleaded with me to stop worrying. 'Boys are slower at reading than girls,' she said.

But during a half-term last year I took him to a 'learning specialist' in London. Redcheeked and anxious, he bravely and diligently went through a series of tests. In the taxi afterwards he cried. 'Did that lady say I was stupid?'

'No' I howled. 'It's your mama who is stupid.'

And then one day Sam picked up *The Haunted Mask*, a creepy thriller from the Goosebumps series. He spent two days reading it. A week later, when I began reading *Five Run Away Together* aloud, he said softly, as if not to hurt my feelings, 'I can read that to myself.' Roald Dahl's *Revolting Rhymes* is lustily read out from the back seat of the car, especially the bit where Little Red Riding Hood whips a pistol from her knickers and kills the big bad wolf.

I'm not saying that reading is what makes life worth living. All my life I've known sociable, neighbourly, humane people, folks who were intelligent, morally competent, kind to people and animals, blessed with good humour, but were not 'book' people. I'm not even saying that I like starting the day with Sustain. All I'm saying is that, even if you never see me on the A143 in a red VW Golf Cabriolet, I believe I have hit the jackpot.

June 6, 1997

178

A GENTLE DEATH

I COME from a family of greedy readers. My grandmother's house twice caught on fire from my grandfather's cigars while he was reading Gibbon's *The History of the Decline and Fall of the Roman Empire*. The surfaces in my father's house were like the Irish rooms in Somerville and Ross, where 'under everything there was something', and the something was always books. My legacy is an instinct for agriculture and a liking for literature. Still, it seemed strange to me that the week my father died he said, 'Sugar, I think you read too much to Sam.'

I looked down at the worn copy of *Oliver Twist*, confused by this unexpected judgment. He went on, 'Every night you read to him in bed. You should take time to tell him stories. Tell him your stories. Tell him our stories. Damn it, the child will never be able to write because he won't have anything in his ear.'

I think of my family stories. Of my father's stories.

How much I need them now; how much I'll need them later. They say that when a person dies, whole worlds die with them. The world that my father takes with him is bigger than most.

So each night I try to tell Sam one of my father's stories. I tell about the floods when the Mississippi burst its banks. I tell about cotton fields and the Depression, about bootleggers and revival meetings.

And I tell him my stories. About riding a horse to school, and fishing for catfish when a water-moccasin wrapped round the paddle. About killing my first snake, a king snake, the farmer's friend, and getting punished because my father had taught me my snakes and he didn't believe in random killing.

Even as I tell the stories I can hear my Pa's editorial voice: 'Keep it simple. Think of de Maupassant, of Chekhov. Remember the details. Remember sequence.' Pa believed that even tragic events had their funny side, that humour was oxygen for the soul. He loved to remind his politician son-in-law that 'if you sought to remove ignorance from the Mississippi legislature, you would no longer have representative government'. He told us: 'The doctors have given me between three and 18 months, so I've decided to take the 18.' All his life he subscribed to the southern philosophy, 'Never let the truth interfere with a good story'.

In a letter my friend Will wrote to my father here at

Wyken, he quoted Martin Luther King's *Letter from a Birmingham Jail:* 'We will have to repent in this generation not merely for the words and actions of the bad people, but for the appalling silence of the good people.' Will continued: 'During a time of acute moral crisis, you did not remain silent, you did not maintain your neutrality.'

The violence and killing in the early 1960s came closer to home with the murder of King's friend Medgar Evers. My father believed he had to take a stand. I remember the tremble in his voice in the small church in Magnolia, Mississippi, when he told the all-white congregation: 'We are all responsible for the death of Medgar Evers.' No bomb threats or burning crosses led him to shrink from the burden of that responsibility.

My father, gentle, brave, kind, came in early April to live with us for what I hoped would turn into a long Indian summer. Three weeks later he died in his sleep in the early hours of the morning. I was sleeping next door, the old baby-listener turned on in case he called in the night. My last words to him were 'I love you'. His last words to me were 'Can you leave my P. D. James on the bed in case I want to read during the night?'

The doctor called it 'the gentle death good men deserve'. As my Pa loved to say: 'The arc of the moral universe is long, but it bends towards justice'.

June 12, 1997

181

STAR TREK ON EARTH

'Mowing hay by hand! Bless their hearts!' An American woman on the train between Bologna and Florence, 1950.

CHANGE, earth-shaking change, is apt to be shadowy. Here on the country's grain prairies, you can still get seasick watching the wind ripple through the barley like ocean waves. Signs offering 'The First New Potatoes' and 'The Last of the Asparagus' lull you into thinking that the harmony of country life is continuous and for ever. Even the riot act between the mother sheep and their toddler lambs sounds like a piece of music as old as the Bible.

And down the road, festive and tidy as a model village, is the Suffolk Show, the annual three-day party of country folk. Here families still look like families, and the Suffolk Punches, Red Poll cattle and Jacob sheep are so clean and sweet you want to hug them.

Women's Institute stalls still sell jam, and burly farmers crowd the Agricultural Mortgage Corporation stand for the beer and sausages they feel are theirs by rights.

Inside the president's tent, tucking into stuffed quail and steamed fennel, are a Church of England bishop, a former Minister of Agriculture, a landowning banker and 40 or so friends of this year's president, Charles Notcutt, whose Suffolk based horticultural business employs more than 1,000 people round the country. This is Trollope country, and only talk of New Labour and the wine – a New Zealand Sauvignon Blanc – tells you that it's Joanna, not Anthony.

A gentle stroll from the president's tent are the farm machinery stands. Bypass these stands and you can return home grateful for the timelessness of rural life. Study the massive John Deeres and Massey Fergusons and you will feel like one of the Borrowers, dwarfed by the gargantuan tractors and drills. Combine harvesters the size of houses now manage 40 tonnes an hour.

Come harvest and more than 200 farmers round England will climb into these space-age machines designed to cocoon the driver from noise, vibration, heat, fumes, dust and jolts. Inside it's as cool and dark as a church, but the altar is a small screen, no larger than a magazine, tracking the machine speed, crop yield and temperature and mapping every foot of the field.

It's *Star Trek* on earth, and it's called precision farming. Last year just a buzzword, now it is reality. Even if the words Global Positioning System, or GPS, don't roll off the tongues of the farmers easing their Grand Cherokees into the vice-president's car park, they soon will.

Prophet and farmer Oliver Walston believes that GPS will revolutionise farming as much as the internal combustion engine did 100 years ago. Farmers will never need to spray a whole field again, costs and pollution will drop dramatically, and in time the combine will glide across the fields by remote control, no driver needed.

Suddenly I feel like the Dennis Skinner of agriculture, stuck in my belief that the land is not a factory and people are not spare parts. And still I know that precision farming is the future. Yield growth has levelled off. Prices are falling. World population is growing rapidly. Who knows if the world will be able to feed itself?

On the next stand I look at Farming On-line. I'm told that the day will come when we'll be able to get digital images of our fields from orbiting satellites via the Internet. We'll be able to see crop density and moisture content and measure the amount of photosynthesis, vital information as we leave the cocoon of the CAP and move into the real world of market forces. Farming by e-mail: info@farmline.com. Bless our hearts.

June 19, 1997

NOT YET BORN AGAIN

IT is Sunday morning and I'm in the kitchen drinking a second cup of coffee and waiting for Alistair Cooke's *Letter From America*. It is a peaceful time. The animals are sleeping and Sam and his father have gone to church. A velvet voice on the radio says, 'And now for a final look at the Sunday papers. The vicar of St Mary the Virgin in Tetbury, Gloucestershire, believes that HRH the Prince of Wales does not go to church regularly enough. The Reverend John Hawthorne says he has not seen the Prince at an act of worship since February'.

There are many things I like about the Prince of Wales. His clothes, for instance. I've always preferred his to hers, actually. I love the beautifully tailored, dense tweeds, the natural way he wears a kilt, the rich blue of the pinstripe suits.

I passionately share his philosophy of farming, although you might not think so if you scrutinised our 850 acres under the plough. I even like those ginger biscuits that come in the discreet box.

And, of course, his garden at Highgrove. Although my admiration is based on photographs and the television programme, I love the sheer exuberance of his planting, the vitality of the structure. It sounds like, 'I danced with the man who danced with the woman who danced with the Prince of Wales,' but I am tickled that the architect the Prince has chosen for his new garden house has just transformed our hideous fifties farm office into a modest Gothic farm office.

So I begin my solitary Sunday ritual, comforted by the knowledge that the Prince also feels that one's spiritual life cannot, will not, be measured by church attendance.

Unlike the Prince of Wales, I come from a long line of religious fanatics, including five great-uncles who were Baptist preachers, and three aunts in their early seventies who have recently been ordained (Episcopal). Spending my Sunday mornings by the radio and working in the garden doesn't come as naturally as you may think.

Nor can I claim a profound ecclesiastical rupture. I am old prayer book, but in favour of women priests. I don't have an evangelical bone in my body, but if you had spent youthful summer evenings at revival meetings being urged to confess your sins and come forward to be born again, you too might prefer the quieter awe of incense and Latin.

No, I'm afraid what has pulled me away from the Church is a mix of excruciating boredom and mild irritation. Nancy Mitford believed that the importance of a good engagement ring is that it gives you something to focus on in church. I now know every flaw in my Ceylonese sapphire, every flicker in the little emerald-cut diamonds, a familiarity honed through many long and banal sermons over the years.

Two years ago our vicar asked us to increase our annual contribution to the church, citing hard times. My good-hearted husband was ready to agree when I began bucking about not subsidising a church that had made bad property deals and now was paying off a bunch of indolent vicars who couldn't handle the idea of women priests.

I proposed a more decorative form of generosity: we'd lime-wash the church and convert its lugubrious grey walls and ceiling into an uplifting bridal white. After a lengthy bureaucratic process, our plan was accepted. Mr Gidney and his daughter, Suffolk's premier lime-washers, transformed the church.

Although my husband felt our bounty should be anonymous, I believe that you should let your light so shine before men that they may see your good works. And the Prince of Wales might note: it seems to make the vicar reluctant to observe that you have not been in a pew since February.

June 26, 1997

DEARLY BELOVED

'All happy families resemble one another but each unhappy family is unhappy in its own way'.
Leo Tolstoy, *Anna Karenina.*

IT is the wedding season and no time to tangle with Tolstoy, but I can't help but think that happy families stick out a mile. They have a uniqueness that is visible, irresistible, and not purchasable. Knowing one genuinely happy family deepens and widens your sense of life. It's like taking your soul to lunch at the *Grand Vefour*. Eureka is marrying into that family.

At least that is how it seems on this walk across the wheat fields from Flamstead Church to Hill Farm. It looks like a scene out of a Bergman movie or *Cold Comfort Farm*: the bride in her long white linen coat, a slender sail in the sea of green; the groom, handsome and manly in his Austrian jacket, guiding his new wife across the fertile fields to her family's home. It is Midsummer's

Day in Hertfordshire, and the sky is a quilt of black and blue.

Friends and family follow, intrepid members of the wedding. I, the countrywoman, find it hard to match the pace of city walkers, Londoners who have mastered power walking. I watch anxiously in the distance as my only child is nearly carried to heaven by his upturned umbrella.

My slower pace gives me time to think about this happy family wedding. Few words in the English language have quite the power of 'Dearly beloved, we are gathered together here in the sight of God, and in the face of this congregation, to join together this man and this woman in holy matrimony.'

Especially nowadays, when a young woman proclaims 'I will' as a consequence of love and respect for a person who seems singularly desirable. How blessed we are to be living in the twilight of the dark ages, when a woman wanted to be a wife because she couldn't possibly conceive of anyone else to be.

This bride, a much-cherished god-daughter of my husband, is in her third year as a qualified doctor. Although today she begins to live with her husband in the holy estate of matrimony, the groom has loved her and comforted her throughout the long years of medical training. They have created a home with the magical address of 'The Top House, Christmas Steps' in Bristol, where they live above the shop: he is a designer and maker of furniture and clocks. Veronica and Robert have not shakily agreed to love and to honour; they have boldly and joyfully affirmed vows that have been years in the making.

So this is a bride who wears no veil, all the better to see the world. Instead she wears a delicate tiara of pearls and gold made for her by the groom. For something old, she wears her great-grandmother's 18th-century diamond paste earrings. For something palest sky blue, a wedding cake made by the bride and groom: he creating the copper columns with silver tendrils, she icing the five layers that signify Blake's Divine Vision.

Even before we drink champagne, partake of the wedding feast, dance reels, eat wedding cake with tea and bid farewell to the couple, who depart for their honeymoon on bicycle, I begin concocting my theory that we are entering an era when marriages will be long-lasting. An era of fewer but better marriages, couples bringing a new degree of commitment, confidence and hope to this age-old setup. Marriage is like democracy: wildly imperfect, but so far nothing is better.

It is the season of weddings and no time to tangle with Philip Larkin, but I think he got it wrong as well, when he wrote 'Man hands on misery to man, it deepens like a coastal shelf...' I reckon that the happiness gene is dominant, and it deepens like the Grand Canyon.

July 10, 1997

THE UNFINISHED SHRINE

ANYBODY seeing the builder's sign nailed to the side of our 18th-century cart shed would make a note to avoid those builders come hell or high water. The sign has been up there nearly two years, and the barn is still in a state of touching dilapidation. Only if you proceed up the stairs 'At Your Own Risk' will you see two discreet Velux windows and a new floor, proof that something got started there.

On top of the black Bechstein piano in the drawing room sit two large leather albums, discreetly embossed with gold initials and dates. The first album begins with ten blank pages, intended for our wedding pictures, which still nestle in a bridal shoebox. On pages 11 to 13, there are photographs of us planting the vineyard, followed by a creamy, blank pause.

In the second album, the birth and babyhood of S.F.C.C. is admirably documented. Alas, by age two, the documentation is replaced with dated fat envelopes that make the album impossible to shut. Even these envelopes cease before his fifth birthday and the rest of his life as seen through the lens of the Canon Sureshot sits in the bottom drawer of the walnut desk.

What we are surrounded by – indeed, what every room in this house is a shrine to – is the unfinished project, the stalled plan, the dreamy vision and the dream *en attendant*. The dinosaur mask book eagerly begun on Boxing Day is stuck at pterodactyl by New Year. The playroom wall is a mosaic of paint colours: John Oliver's Rameses Red, Fired Earth's Quiet Green, Farrow and Ball's Ballroom Blue. The plan to turn this into a family room is on hold until a commitment can be made.

In my head throbs Elizabeth Bishop's villanelle about losing: 'The art of losing isn't hard to master; so many things seem filled with the intent to be lost that their loss is no disaster.' In my version the verb to lose is replaced by to finish. So many things seem filled with the intent to go unfinished that I dare not count the incomplete as disaster.

The converted cart shed was supposed to be my 'Vita Sackville West tower', a place where I could pull myself together and finish something. But as soon as there was a glimmer of light coming through the roof I began to think: 'What do I want to do in here? I've already got a drawer full of unfinished novels'. 'Art is too long and life is too short', I told my husband, 'Let's put a ping-pong table there instead.'

To console myself I claim that I'm merely the acute form of one of the chronic ailments of our age. We all move onto something new before the old thing is done. We are besotted with beginnings. Sometimes I don't regret the unfinished project. I am relieved that the grapevine stencils never made it onto the kitchen walls, that the chicken wire for topiary became a patio for the guinea pig. There is space in the attic for my Linguaphone sets of Russian and Italian just in case I ever lose the use of both legs.

But in order for civilisation to progress, each generation needs to improve on the preceding one. I want Sam to finish his Robin Hood exhibition, started during half-term. I'd like the Meccano bridge on the card-table in the hall to finally be complete. I want the Sir Francis Drake prayer about beginnings being just great but the 'continuing until it be thoroughly finished yields the true glory' drummed into his little head.

To make myself feel less haphazard, I've decided to finish something everyday. Today I wrapped for mailing to my sister the twelve William Morris needlepoint kits for chair seats, including the first one that is a little shop worn. I edited the video cupboard and created a Postman Pat and Fireman Sam box for the village playgroup. Of course I may not get to the post office or the playgroup this week but it won't be a disaster.

July 17, 1997

THE OX IN THE DITCH

JAMES BOYLE knows as much about what people want as a hog knows about Sunday. If he has a lick of sense, he'll start trying to find out.

In case the name doesn't ring a bell, Mr Boyle is the Radio 4 controller who is due to announce his 1998 programme changes any day now. BBC insiders gloomily mutter about plans to 'tuck *Farming Today* into the *Today* programme, delete the farm reports and feature environmental stories'. It's a euphemistic way of saying *Farming Today* is doomed. The early matinal report on the farming business will vanish from our lives as seamlessly as the grey partridge, wild cornflowers, hedgerows and family farms.

We will no longer begin our day at ten past six with Balzacian accounts of the rise in pig sales to Japan (up 157% due to foot-and-mouth disease in Taiwan), the fall in milk yields due to the cold, wet weather, the Cattle Passport scheme for all cattle destined for the food chain, or Sainsbury's stand against genetically modified foods. Which is to say: there will no longer be a daily, useful, vital link between the British people and their countryside.

It's not the first time the BBC has thought of dumping *Farming Today*. Back in 1990, when I heard of its imminent demise, I launched a 'One Farmer and Her Dog' petition campaign, sending pages of the petition to everyone I knew with a gentle hint that it would be grand if they return it with 20 or 30 signatures. It seemed pretty dozy stuff after storming the Pentagon, and I don't have a lot of faith in petitions, but in the end I sent a few thousand signatures to Broadcasting House. Even on a morning when all I want to do is go back to sleep, I've felt a tender pride on hearing those words 'Welcome to *Farming Today*'.

Old friends can't understand why I get so het up about this radio programme. They think it's a mighty little cause if you've tilted at the bigger windmills of Freedom and Equality and Justice. I reckon it's a very big cause.

When the BBC decides to dump *Farming Today*, it is shoving the countryside and rural issues further and further to the edge, making it the fringe of the fringe. It is saying that farming and conservation issues aren't important, aren't prime time. The 11 million, or 25% of the people in this country who live in rural parts, a silent, modest, pretty ordinary minority, don't excite the BBC as much as exotic, urban minorities. In this the BBC is reinforcing a worrying and unnecessary political trend which is setting town against countryside.

But there is another reason why *Farming Today* is a cause to fight for. Take it off the air and you are isolating farmers even further. They don't just lose touch with the state-of-the-art crop reports and the vagaries of CAP legislation. They lose access to new ideas and changing perspectives that can make them better guardians of the environment.

I'm a farmer who believes that farmers have been far from perfect guardians of the countryside. A farmer who believes we desperately need a food and farming policy that serves the public interest and encourages a safe, sustainable farming system.

I also believe that even if we have the technology to check out Mars, earthly civilisation depends on a few inches of topsoil for its very existence. Wanting and knowing how to take care of the earth is in the hands of those who farm it. The faithful touchstone of these yearnings is *Farming Today*.

And look, just in case you agree with me, I'd be grateful if you'd write to Mr Boyle as fast as you can, at Broadcasting House, London W1A 1AA. He really wants to get a feel for what the people want. I reckon he's really a good man who cares what the people want. Cross my heart and catch a hog.

July 24, 1997

IV
Harvest

BANK NOTES

A FEW years ago a new bank opened in our market town. Proudly called the Farmers and Merchants Bank, it's run rather like the Wine Society. In order to open an account, a potential depositor must be recommended by a customer of the bank. Otherwise you have to submit to an extensive credit check.

But once you are in, you are trusted. Pens aren't chained to the counter. Instead of bouncing your cheques, the bank gives you a telephone call and tells you what the situation is. Just off the lobby are nice loos, a godsend since the Suffolk Hotel closed. And in the back of the bank there is a zinc bar where you can get a cappuccino and have a look at the *Financial Times* or *The Economist*.

Everybody knows each other, and the tellers have all been here since the bank opened. When the asparagus season opens, a bundle of Suffolk asparagus is set aside for every customer. Elaine telephones you to let you know when picking starts.

Okay. Maybe I went over the top with the bit about the cappuccinos. Maybe the asparagus idea blew it. But if you fell for it, you probably think I've done one of the crummiest things a person can do: restored your faith in banks only to find it was a hoax.

Perhaps hoax is a little harsh. Let's say dream. How earth-shaking can it be to dream of a bank where people know you and you know them? I can still remember when that was normal.

When I lived in London my bank was the Pont Street National Westminster. Mr Maskell was my bank manager but Miss Cooper was helpful and attentive as well. It was my policy always to dress in my Sunday best when meeting with Mr Maskell because I wanted him to feel that his faith in me was well placed. I also took Adam, my well-mannered labrador, to these appointments, because his well-being depended on my skilful negotiations during lean times.

Truthfully, no one was more thrilled on my behalf than Mr Maskell when I told him that I was engaged.

'He's a Suffolk farmer, Mr Maskell. Not rich but...'

'But solid?' came the hopeful voice.

'Yes, Mr Maskell. Solid.'

A few years after I moved to the country dear Mr Maskell retired. Then the Pont Street NatWest was retired as well. I transferred my account to the Bury St Edmunds branch where, five years on, I know no one and no one knows me. Indeed, when I recently asked the name of my bank manager, I was told that there are several 'account managers' but no one bank manager. It's not that I believe in hierarchy, but I feel an old-fashioned discomfort when I deposit my money into a mousehole with no name.

And this is the pattern: fewer branches, anonymous service, and more and more leaflets in the lobby describing the burgeoning number of 'products' the bank offers.

A farmer who thinks only in terms of annual production, rather than in terms of a long-term system of caring for his land and maintaining its fertility and ecological health, is slowly smothering the goose that lays the profitable eggs. Banks which believe that short-term profits are the number one goal are practising homicidal economics.

Meanwhile, we sure could use a Farmers and Merchants Bank here in Suffolk. When the price of wheat drops from £130 to £80 a tonne in a ten-month period, you like to think you have a friendly bank where the folks know you and like your dog.

July 31, 1997

LOVE STORY

A FEW years ago, William Goldman wrote a book about Hollywood and screenwriting. His own credits include *Butch Cassidy and the Sundance Kid* and *Marathon Man* so I reckon he knows a thing or two. But what I remember is his advice on adapting a story for film. Before you begin writing you have to know the answer to two questions: what is the story about? And what's the story *really* about?

These questions ring in my head as we drive home after a lunch party held in honour of Cosmo and Grania, old friends of my husband's family. They came to our wedding, rejoiced in the birth of our son, encouraged the planting of the vines and were our most faithful customers in the vineyard restaurant in the early days when we didn't have – or need – a book for reservations.

I suspect Cosmo was sad when we ended the shoot at Wyken. He was aghast when he learned I had thrown out my husband's I Zingari tie during the editing phase of early marriage. He gently tries to soften my heart on the subject of Harrow where Nevills and Carlisles have gone for generations.

But, above all, Cosmo and Grania are like members of a family that is like a clear lake in which we can see the reflections of ourselves. Their pleasure, curiosity and approval give us energy and confidence.

So when the invitation arrived requesting our company at a celebration of Cosmo's 90th birthday and Grania's birthday, along with their 63rd wedding anniversary, we felt like we were going home.

Friends and family gathered at midday at the Army and Navy Club in Pall Mall. We drank champagne, ate well and listened to reflections on Cosmo and Grania. I realised what a long and true love story theirs is.

It began 70 years ago when Cosmo was a cadet at Sandhurst and Grania a 14-year-old schoolgirl, the daughter of one of Cosmo's instructors. The lanky, elegant young officer fell in love with the slender, blue-eyed schoolgirl, and against all barriers of reason, they made their silent vows of love and patience. Cosmo left Sandhurst an officer in the Royal Fusiliers, honoured with the King's Medal, the Sword of Honour and a romantic destiny.

In those days an officer under the age of 30 had to obtain permission to marry. As soon as Grania was 18 Cosmo made his request to his Commanding Officer. He was refused. Dramatically – and very un-English – he transferred from the 2nd battalion to the 1st – which was in India, where a more kindly commanding officer gave him permission to marry.

Eighteen months later he returned to England and, in 1934, on the bride's 21st birthday, they were married.

After a honeymoon fishing on the Isle of Skye, they returned to India where Cosmo joined General Wavell's staff and Grania began a nomadic life that would lead to 23 moves in 24 years. She gave birth to a son and a daughter; nurtured the families of the men in her husband's regiment and learned to fly. In 1943 they returned to England and a year later, Cosmo was given command of the 2nd Battalion Devonshire regiment to lead them in the assault on Normandy on D-Day.

Three months later Cosmo was badly wounded. He spent two years recovering, then went on duty to the United Nations in New York. He returned to the Fusiliers but a heart attack forced his retirement. Grania again nursed him and taught him to paint, launching him on a very successful second career.

So what is the story? A romantic tale about two people with stamina, ethics and courage. What is the real story? That we are so absorbed in our picayune activities that we do not tap into the deep, rich lives close to us, lives with a completeness uncommon and unknown in our generation. We should listen. Then we might hear the *real* story.

August 14, 1997

MULE DAYS

My grandmother had little faith in people's capacity for change. To prove her faithlessness she would always point to cousin Hazel who was 'born lazy'. Despite her indolence, Hazel managed to go to junior college, take the Illinois Central to Chicago, work in the advertising department of Marshall Field, get a husband, get divorced and come back home. She moved in with Uncle Edgar and Aunt Sissy, and spent the rest of her life sitting on the front porch reading books by Taylor Cauldwell and Frank Yerby. 'You can take a donkey travelling but it won't come back a horse,' my grandmother opined. She'd have scoffed at the miles of shelves devoted to self-help books in Books Etc. She'd have advised the Duchess of York to hang on to her size 16 dresses. She even doubted the fervour of Born Again Christians whom she suspected of simply trying to wriggle out of the motley mess of everyday life.

For her children and grand-children this legacy of being stuck with who you are was a terrible burden. It went against everything we were taught at school. Each morning in assembly we were reminded of 'the never-ending task of self improvement' (Emmerson), of man elevating 'his life by conscious endeavour' (Thoreau).

But the most stirring lessons in self-improvement came from Mr Pichotino, my speech teacher, who propounded the Cary Grant theory. 'I pretended to be somebody I wanted to be, and I finally became that person,' Mr Grant said. 'Or he became me. Or we met at some point. It's a relationship.'

It was the Cary Grant philosophy that lead me to get rid of my southern accent and to act nicer than I felt. I have to say that, up until now, it has been a pretty good method.

In fact, it wasn't until I was standing in the hot sun at Uttoxeter Race course a couple of Sundays ago, that I began to hear my grandmother's doubts ringing in my ears. I had dragged my family half way across England to attend the annual British Mule Day. Nobody had wanted to go and it required some bucking and snorting to get them there. Lorraine Travis, secretary and Joan of Arc of the British Mule Society, had asked me to present the prizes. But I was really there to check out the mules.

You see, despite a fancy education, an English accent and good table manners, I'm happiest on the back of a mule. That's where I spent my formative years and, like cousin Hazel realising that the front porch is where she feels true to herself, I've come to understand that I belong on a mule.

In case you aren't sure about mules, I'll tell you. They are highly intelligent – smarter than horses – and, when well-trained and kindly handled, they are obliging, kind, patient, intrepid, calm, tolerant, sensible, loyal and affectionate. A cross between a male donkey and a female horse, mules have the body of a horse with the trim of a donkey: long ears, short thin mane and eyes that are full of goodness. Their reputation for being stubborn is all wrong. Like children, they are mean and stubborn only when they've been brought up badly.

At British Mule Day all the mules behaved impeccably, especially Muffin, a black-and-white mule who used to work cattle in Wyoming, and two beautiful piebald mules belonging to His Honour Sir Sanderson Temple from Lancashire.

Come next spring I'll have a mule of my own. In the evenings I'll ride over the farm and check the crops. Mules are such smooth rides you don't really need a saddle, nor do they need to be shod. And if this corner of Suffolk starts looking like an advertisement for Jack Daniels, well, I reckon that's a blessing.

August 21, 1997

207

DOG TALK

WHEN I came to Wyken as a bride there weren't any dogs. Of course Howard, the gamekeeper, had his dogs – spaniels – that lived in an outdoor kennel behind his cottage, but Adam, my labrador and dowry, was the first dog to sleep in front of the fire in the hall for 40 years.

Adam's transition from town dog to gundog was not seamless, but he would quiver with excitement when he saw the gun. He proved to be fairly adept at picking up pheasants. His only problem in that field was a yearning to make friends with the other dogs. After the social life of Putney Heath, the country seemed a lonely place.

But Adam's great quality was that he was well-educated. When I was growing up, my sister and I were each allowed our own dog on our ninth birthday. The rule was that you could choose your pup and train it yourself. If your dog chased cars, stole from the kitchen, killed chickens, or chewed anything other than bones, then you were punished. So we took training seriously and enjoyed our limited tyranny.

We spent hours teaching them to 'sit', 'hi on', 'charge', 'heel', 'play dead' and 'stay'. We made balls of yarn filled with pins to teach them to retrieve in the most delicate manner. We never yelled at our dogs and we spared the lash because it breaks their spirit. Years later I patiently applied these same methods (sans yarn balls) to Adam.

Now we have a new dog, a yellow labrador named Fanny. We chose her when she was a week old, visited her every Sunday and at eight weeks brought her home. At nine months she is admired for her fine looks and her calm nature. But I seem to have lost my touch for training

I think I know what that problem is. For eight years now I've been a woman under the influence. Between the training of Adam and the arrival of Fanny, I've had a child, and Dr Spock and Penelope Leach have filled me with the desire to be understanding, devoted, patient, motherly and kind, an all-pervasive emphasis on good parenting. So when Fanny chews Sam's Doc Martens I gently scold her: 'It's not you who is bad but what you've done that is bad.' When she finally returns after 20 minutes chasing a rabbit, I ask: 'Do you want to talk about it?' When she comes into the house wet from a long swim in the pool I remind her of the buddy system: 'Sugar, it's not safe to swim alone.' I worry that I'm not giving her enough quality time.

I am not a lone sufferer in this new era of canine liberalism. The Dorling Kindersley *Dog Breed*

Handbook, published in 1996, advises puppy owners to 'organise weekly puppy parties to help your labrador develop necessary social skills'. I can scarcely organise play dates for my eight-year-old son, but I guiltily invited Fanny's sister over for the day. Alas, the sleek black Cosette had never seen chickens strolling in an apple orchard and the only social skill Fanny acquired was a passion for chasing chickens that hitherto she had ignored.

Two dead chickens later, I decided to follow a course that is discouraged by Drs Leach and Spock. I tied a feathered carcass round Fanny's pale neck and did not look into her soft, bewildered eyes for 24 hours. Sam threatened to report me to the RSPCA, but I told him if Fanny killed another chicken he wouldn't get any pocket money for three months.

And, reader, it worked. Now the chickens don't even bother to step aside when Fanny walks into the orchard. In fact she's suddenly become so obedient that I'm thinking about writing a book on training a good country dog. And if anybody shows up here to complain, I'll just whisper 'Sick 'em'.

August 28, 1997

THE DUCHESS FROM BALTIMORE

FRANK BALDRY, head cowman at Wyken for 30 years, divided people into two categories: those who 'ain't never left the parish' and those 'who'd been out of the parish'.

I've been chewing over this parochial division because I have lived in Suffolk for 11 years now but have never been to Ipswich. My train stops there *en route* to London and I've bought shelves at the Sainsbury's Homebase on its outskirts, but Ipswich proper is unknown to me.

My lack of curiosity is odder still because Ipswich was the scene of a turning point in English history. On October 27, 1936, an undefended divorce petition was heard at Ipswich Assizes and a decree nisi was awarded with costs against a Mr Ernest Simpson. Thus the first stage of Edwards VIII's abdication began.

When I was growing up, the Duke and Duchess of Windsor were still described as 'the greatest love story of the century'. To a young girl looking at their photographs in *LIFE* magazine, the wistful, boyish man who would have been King of England, and his twice-divorced American wife with her stern head and large jewellery, did not look romantic.

But years later I became fascinated by the story. I devoured Frances Donaldson's book *Edward VIII* and picked up copies of *The Heart Has Its Reasons* and *A King's Story* for 50p in secondhand book shops. I knew the world the Duchess came from, a Southern world that valued birth and breeding more than money and success.

When I came to Wyken, my husband showed me a bundle of letters addressed to his cousin who bought the estate in 1921. The letters were written eight years earlier by the Prince of Wales when they were together at Magdalen, Oxford. The Prince's chief pleasures in those years were shooting and hunting. His chief displeasure was schoolwork. Although genetically the Prince was almost pure German, after spending the summer of 1913 there with relatives he wrote: 'Germany is the most ghastly country'.

Now I've gone one step further and acquired the ultimate edition of their history: Sotheby's two-volume catalogue titled simply *The Duke and Duchess of Windsor*. Nearly 1,200 pages, it lists more than 3,000 lots that are to be auctioned in New York in 18 sessions over nine days in September.

This sale includes every possession they inherited or collected during their long, acquisitive lives: paintings, furniture, silver, private papers, towels, sheets, all her clothes, all his clothes, shoes, handbags, the desk where Edward signed away his throne, their wedding album with photographs by Cecil Beaton, a small, white box containing a piece of their wedding cake. It is all being sold by Mohamed Al Fayed who bought the Duke and Duchess's Paris residence and its entire contents after the Duchess's death in 1986. Better known as the owner of Harrods, a London shop where a cost-conscious Mrs Simpson regularly bought cream-coloured candles, Mr Al Fayed plans to donate the proceeds of the sale to his charity.

Still, perhaps the English people should now acknowledge their gratitude to Wallis Warfield Simpson of Baltimore. By capturing the heart of Edward VIII, she served this country well. As Duke and Duchess of Windsor they lived their pleasure-loving, ultra-rich, trivial lives divided between New York and France, while George VI and his family provided the steadiness and greater intellectual capacity the country needed.

All the same, I'm sad that the house on the edge of Bois de Boulogne will not be kept intact as a museum. The ersatz palace is a compelling portrait of a time and place, a monument to two people who had style and time and loved stuff. I may yet get to Ipswich but I do not think the Assizes will have the same power.

September 4, 1997

THE PRINCESS OF LONGING

AT four in the morning the telephone rang and a deep Southern voice said: 'I'm so sorry, just so, so sorry'. It was my friend Ben Harman in Texas, who has never understood the five-hour time difference. Thus I learned that Diana, Princess of Wales had died in a car crash in Paris only moments earlier.

I remember where I was when President Kennedy was killed. And Martin Luther King and then Robert Kennedy. My mother called it 'the age of grief', and we attended its funerals in our living room in front of our black-and-white television.

Years later, on a visit to England, I felt I had entered the age of joy when I attended the wedding of the Prince and Princess of Wales, again in front of a television. I wept softly as the bride walked up the aisle, supporting her proud but frail father. I wept as the couple said their vows.

Although I am closer in age to HRH the Prince of Wales than to the Princess, it was her life that became a kind of backdrop of those years: her transformation from pudgy Sloane to slender, regal Princess; her transition from shy wife to confident mother; the change from glamourous idol to fragile woman trapped by bulimia and a loveless marriage.

When *The Sunday Times* began to serialise *Diana, Her True Story*, my husband cancelled the paper. Three years passed before it was allowed back in our house. Although my husband and I have different views on politics, history, food, religion, education and farming, the only real rows we've ever had were about Charles and Diana. He defended the traditional, emotionally contained, diligent Prince, while I stood up for the wronged, needy, lonely, loving, emotional Princess. I admired her immaculate manners, her discipline, her fastidious appearance and sense of duty. I believed in her kindness.

Occasionally, my loyalty waned. I regretted her interest in astrology, colonic irrigation, shopping, Danielle Steele, New Age quests and Phil Collins. Still I stuck by her. Until the *Panorama* interview. Suddenly the Princess had become too American for me. Or had I become too English? I could not bear the confessions, the revelations, the heavily rimmed eyes. I turned against both the Prince and Princess for revealing to the world things that, for the sake of their sons, should have stayed unsaid.

I nursed my disappointment and cynicism until she died. I turned down an invitation to view the Princess's dresses at Christie's. When I saw a photograph of the kiss on a cover of Paris Match, my chief regret was that she hadn't fallen in love with a heart surgeon. I'd managed to forget that the human soul, even the soul of a princess, craves joy, that joy is necessary to health and happiness.

Now that it is too late, I wish I had been more generous, more understanding. More American. Words such as icon and saint make me uneasy, except in the modest belief that saints are sinners who kept on going. No, the epitaph that comes to my mind is simply that she made a success out of her difficult, lonely life, that she succeeded in a way that meant something to thousands, to a people, a nation, to humanity. Something that Ralph Waldo Emerson understood when he wrote that success is:

> To leave the world a bit better, whether by a
>   healthy child, a garden path or a
>   redeemed social condition;
> To know even one life has breathed easier
>   because you have lived...

September 11, 1997

216

THE REMEDY FOR DYING

EVERY week my sister and I talk on the telephone. She calls these conversations 'progress reports'. She tells me about life insurance policies, investments, evaluations, bills outstanding. All summer long she has been emptying our parents' house. Most weekends, she goes there with her husband in his jeep Cherokee and they fill it with things that are then distributed to my nephews, friends, our father's church, the homeless shelter, the hospice. This morning she called to say that the house is now on the market. Empty, freshly painted, all new carpets. 'Hallelujah!' she said.

This is what my sister is good at: getting on with things, collecting documents, filing forms, keeping records, insisting on clarification. She is executor of our father's estate, efficient, organised and thorough. When she sends me papers that require my signature, she highlights each space in neon yellow so that I will complete the form accurately. She wants things settled.

217

'Closure' is that term she uses, a word that derives from that real-estate business but which now seems to apply to realms emotional.

But closure is the one thing that I dread. Walking through the house on my last trip, looking in my mother's room, my father's room, the book-lined study, the living room filled with furniture that had been my grandfather's, I found it hard to say, 'I want this,' 'I'll take that.' What I wanted was for everything to stay intact, including the shabbiness that settles on a house whose ageing inhabitants have ceased to see faded and worn carpets, wallpaper peeling from walls, kitchen cupboards that don't quite shut.

In the end I settled on what was portable: quilts, some pictures, a few boxes of books. The other volumes – a truck load – are now in Tennessee filling the shelves of a library whose books were washed away in last year's floods.

'Don't you want these?' my sister asked, pulling open a drawer full of my school reports ('she lives in her own world', 'could try harder'), essays, short stories, a few attempts at scrapbooks, including my collection of fans from the funeral home in our small town. On one side a picture of Jesus with shoulder-length hair, gazing on a cloudy night sky, on the other a biblical quote printed above the address and telephone number of the Lackey Memorial Funeral Home. FOR DUST THOU ART AND

UNTO DUST SHALL THOU RETURN. *Telephone Night or Day.* THE LORD GIVETH AND THE LORD TAKETH AWAY. *Funeral Policies Give Peace of Mind.* YEA, THOUGH I WALK THROUGH THE VALLEY OF THE SHADOW OF DEATH I WILL FEAR NO EVIL. *Consider Your Loved Ones: Make a Will: We Notarize Free of Charge.*

The fans are attached to wooden handles like the flat sticks used by doctors to hold down tongues. 'These might be collectors items now that everything is air-conditioned,' I suggested. 'I don't think so,' my sister replied.

We had identical childhoods, country girls who gathered eggs, helped with the milking, caressed our newborn calves, fished for catfish using chicken necks for bait. I turned into the dreamy wanderer. She stayed behind, candid and practical.

The estate cannot be settled until the house is sold, she tells me. Cremated ashes should not be spread in gardens or under plants, especially roses. Too much calcium kills them.

The newly painted, empty house signals the end of the revolving doors of childhood. Like the collection of funeral fans or my shabby teddy, it has acquired an inflated value. 'Remember this,' my sister says, 'the only remedy for dying is living.' I would say 'Hallelujah,' if only I could.

September 18, 1997

219

ARTICULATE TAWNY OWL

ON a hot day in August, Sam and I were out commiserating with the sheep when we saw what looked like a log in their water trough. We gasped when we saw it was a tawny owl up to its neck in the water. At first we thought he was a clever fellow trying to get cool. Then we realised he couldn't move.

I ran down to the farm workshop to fetch the welding gloves while Sam went off to the grain store to pick up his cage of newly captured mice. Our plan was to lift the owl from his watery prison and release a mouse at the same time, providing freedom and supper in one fell swoop. Alas, the mouse scurried to his salvation while the owl trudged about, aimless and forlorn.

'I reckon he's too waterlogged to fly,' Sam said as I carried the sodden creature home. We set up our nursing home for ailing birds: sheets of newspaper laid out in the pantry, a bowl of water, a makeshift perch and, for a cage, a large Rubbermaid laundry basket placed over the invalid like a dome. We've rescued more than a dozen birds this way, giving them a peaceful few days to recover. We have a 95% success rate, but this was our first owl.

I called the Hawk and Owl Trust. They were helpful but not hopeful. Still, he began to look a little more alive when I set up my 12-inch desk fan in front of the laundry basket. He turned towards it and leaned sideways in that sweet, cock-eyed owl position. The gentle breeze restored him and in the dead of night he devoured the raw pieces of chicken Sam had procured from the restaurant.

His presence made us all happy. Sam proudly showed him to his friends. My husband studied his intricate wing structure. I checked on him night and day – which is how I knew he was getting better and was probably longing for that little patch of blue that prisoners call the sky. One evening at dusk, we gathered together and took him back to the field where we had found him. We wished him luck, thanked him for his company and gently launched him on his way. He rewarded us with a long, silent, timeless, confident flight, finally disappearing into the embrace of a worldly oak tree.

The image of the owl, nurtured to health, soaring free, at first seemed a sign, even to someone like myself who isn't big on signs. But I thought it was an image I could latch on to as I sewed on name-tapes, shortened trousers and went on expeditions with Sam to Cambridge to buy his tuck box and laundry bag. Sam was my articulate tawny owl about to soar to the oak tree of prep school where he would be free from the constant gaze of a mother's concern and attention. The laundry basket of home would be lifted and he could begin to fly.

He has now been away one week. The first two days I felt that I'd misread the sign: I was the owl flying to freedom. I was giddy with my new liberation. My husband was in London, my child was safe and sound and surrounded by the friends an only child yearns for. I even felt like sending the dog to camp so my freedom could be complete.

And then it was like the line in Scott Fitzgerald's *The Crack Up*, where he talks about recovering from a long bout of despair and then, suddenly, feeling better: 'And as soon as I heard the news I cracked like an old plate'. On day three I cracked, not decisively like a plate, but softly, quietly, sadly. It happened early in the evening, when I realised that I really liked having supper at six o'clock and talking about Liverpool versus Manchester. That the ritual of the bedtime story was not my duty but my happiness. That nurturing my tawny owl called Sam was the best and the longest job I'd ever had.

September 25, 1997

A CULTIVATED LIFE

My earliest vow to myself was this: that I would never again live in the middle of nowhere. My dream, nourished in a childhood reached by gravel roads, was always to live on a street with sidewalks. That way, I figured, whenever you walked out of the front door, you would be always somewhere.

So I began my married life in the country with a settled fatalism. With each step – taking over the management of the farm, planting of the vines, birth of a child – the exciting, well-paved worlds of London and Paris became ever more remote. Unopened copies of *The New Yorker* piled up like haystacks as their pages became as mysterious as an obscure foreign language.

Still, there was one worldly patch I watched with envy and fascination: the beautiful coppery red thatched cottage down the road from the vineyard. Surrounded by corn fields and protected from the narrow Langham road by high hedges, only I could see this fiery jewel from my secret vantage point among the vines. Sometimes I glimpsed visitors to the cottage, elegant, interesting-looking people who did not wear Barbours. I followed the progress of the controversial and exquisite barn being built next to the cottage, stained a weathered grey, roofed in old tiles, a beautiful rebuke to the creosoted, corrugated structures preferred by Suffolk farmers and planners.

Eventually, I learned that the cottage belonged to Jorn Langberg, a Dane who had come to England in the 1950s, studied at St Martin's, and become chief couturier and head of Christian Dior in London where he lived during the week. I relished every exotic detail. When I was told one clear November weekday that the huge number of cars surrounding the house were there for the funeral of his close friend, I felt as sad as I might for someone I knew.

Maybe that is why, on December 23, eight and a half months pregnant and *en route* to collect our Christmas goose, I suddenly stopped the car, knocked on the ancient oak door of the cottage and introduced myself to the tall, handsome, silver-haired, ageless man who answered. Nervously, I invited him to join us for Christmas Eve, or Christmas Day, or Boxing Day. With great tact, he declined but invited us to dinner on Epiphany. Thus began a friendship that is one of my greatest sources of pride and pleasure.

Like Lord Merlin in *The Pursuit of Love*, Jorn is epicurean, generous, whimsical, fastidious, cultivated: the urbane foreigner in a country setting who becomes the repository for the most personal feelings and creative ideas of his fellow villagers. In no time, Jorn was also my mentor. When I limewashed the Hall, I spent days trying to mix 'Langberg-Suffolk Red'. When I converted our 400-year-old barn, I stained the new timbers Northern Tundra, the weathered grey of his barn. The fence round the pool is a version of Jorn's crinkle-crankle wall. Despite my faithful flattery, Wyken is Tobacco Road and Jorn's miniature estate, Hillwatering, is Vaux-le-Vicomte.

For the past six years, Jorn's contribution to country life in this part of East Anglia has been even more tangible. In late September, he holds an exhibition of the best of British artists. The pictures fill his barn, house, outbuildings and gardens. Each year, something new is added – portraits last year, garden sculpture this. To art-loving country dwellers who feel less and less inclined to journey to London, the exhibition is a cultural and social godsend. And every year I buy a picture. I reckon I pay for it with the money I save on travel. And the truth is, nothing soothes a vagabond's heart like good friends and good pictures, earthbound pleasures.

October 2, 1997

LIFE'S END AT LAND'S END

This shows imagination, but one senses a deliberate attempt to appear original.

THOSE haughty words, written in red in the margin, were a teacher's rebuke to the 12-year-old Colette when she wrote that she did not agree 'with those who called autumn a decline'. I'm on Colette's side: autumn is not an ending, it is a beginning. I never feel so alive and born again as I do in the sharp warmth and amber sunshine of October, tart apples and pears dropping onto the ground, the first pumpkin and leek risotto, the first blackberry and apple crumble, the ceremony of putting on a sweater when I go out to feed the chickens.

It's also the beginning of the grape harvest. Every other morning, I prowl through the vineyard, picking a bucketful of grapes from several rows. Using a potato masher, I crush them, stir the juice and put a few drops on the prismatic tip of a small, black instrument called a refractometer. Holding it up to the sunlight, I look for the black shadow that falls across a scale and tells me the sugar level of the grapes. This year's crop is small, hurt by the killer frost in April and the rains in June, but the survivors record a perfect and punctual ripeness.

By the time I'm back home, another crop has arrived: catalogues, now as much a part of autumn as conkers and Michaelmas daisies. Every day brings new offerings. Yesterday it was Hawkshead and Land's End, this morning a bumper crop, Racing Green, Boden and Peruvian Connection. Looking at these catalogues you would think that everyone on this island lives in the country and owns a faded petrol pump, a chocolate labrador, outdoor kennels, a stretch of river and has need of poachers' jackets, fishermen's rollnecks and moleskin jeans.

Literature has not caught up with the role of these catalogues in our lives. In Aga sagas, no heroine sits by the warmth of her cream-coloured Aga with the latest Boden catalogue, deliberating over the leopardskin jeans – 'a little adventurous without being silly'. Pages of Past Times are not used to get the fire started. No one writes that 'the sleeveless sweater in fine merino wool from Hawkshead was perfect for evening spent grass-casting a soft rod with an overweighted line'. How exotic *A Dance to the Music of Time* seems, the age of French champagne, old roses and silk, in this era of Oregon pinot noirs, organic vegetables and mail-order polar fleece.

Catalogues, like litigation and hypochondria, are so American that it is hard to believe that they are now as much a part of English life as the Proms, the London Library and Radio 4. I remember trips back home when I could scarcely unpack before beginning to devour the catalogues my mother would save for me. She used to say, 'If you ever write about these years, be sure to describe the ruffle of pages turning during all our heart-to-heart talks.' She generously offered me the title *Life's End at Land's End.*

Even now I pore over the pages of each catalogue, making extravagant lists: the navy and plum sweater, the sheepskin-collared jacket. I fold down pages to come back to. As the days pass, I reduce my wants and feel instantly virtuous. I find comfort in the privacy of my greed.

When I finally place my order, I'm as impatient as a child waiting for the delivery. The parcels are like presents. I rejoice at their arrival, and then I carefully put the treasures away. I do not wear the cherry red poacher's jacket for picking grapes or chopping wood. I do not feed the sheep in my herringbone Capris. I save these country clothes for dressing up to go somewhere. For trips to town. For occasions when I make a deliberate attempt to appear original.

October 9, 1997

FAMILY FEUDS

NOTHING defines a family like its feuds. The family I come from nursed a feud that began under Roosevelt, flared up under the Kennedys and wore out with Jimmy Carter. Our family motto is 'forgive but do not forget'.

Still, my southern Gothic roots did not prepare me for the rich tapestry of feuds hanging in the family into which I married, feuds that made every family gathering as tricky as Arab peace talks, feuds which kept the family riven for three generations.

I became aware of the most dramatic feud when, as a bride on holiday in the South of France, I went with my husband to Château de la Garoupe, a beautiful Italianate château and garden on Cap d'Antibes. He was hoping to explore the gardens while the owner, his cousin, was away in Switzerland. We spent a long afternoon trespassing the avenues of ancient olive trees, gazing in the distance at the Alpes Maritimes.

As nervous as a spy, I photographed the parterre of

rosemary, santolina and lavender and the terrace planted with orange trees and night-scented jasmine. Our hearts pounded as we raced down the 130 marble steps that led to the sea. La Garoupe was the lifelong passion of my husband's great-grandmother. For two years, she scoured the Riviera from Monaco to Toulon before settling, in 1904, on this slender peninsula on the eastern tip of Cap d'Antibes. She claimed she wanted 'just enough land for a nice garden', and spent the next 30 years creating her 100 acre paradise.

My knowledge of La Garoupe was gleaned from memoirs and biographies. My husband's great-grandparents spent their winters there, but his pragmatic great-grandmother was the first to let her house to summer tenants. The blue-haired Lady Mendl came first, followed by Cole Porter, who took the house for many years. It was the peace and beauty of La Garoupe that inspired Gerald and Sara Murphy to buy the property next door that they would call Villa America, providing the sensuous, doomed model for F. Scott Fitzgerald's *Tender is the Night*.

Then, in 1934, La Garoupe's chatelaine died, followed a year later by her husband. When the will was read, it emerged that the estate had not been left to the eldest son, as decreed by the cast-iron expectations of primogeniture, but to his sister Fay. My husband's grandfather was shocked and disappointed. Brother and sister never spoke again. As they were both serious, indeed passionate, gardeners, their mutual loss was great. As feuds go, this was a particularly good one: a wild and romantic estate purchased and created by a headstrong heiress and left to a daughter who loved it with equal passion. I relished stories of Fay's sons travelling to La Garoupe on the *Train Bleu* from their English prep schools each Christmas. I found myself taking sides, predictably the wrong side.

But time changes everything, even La Garoupe. Over the years, the 100 acres dwindled to a mere, priceless 25. Fay's heir, her younger son, died childless. And last night, at dinner with cousins, my husband learned that La Garoupe had been sold. The buyer? Boris Yeltsin.

No one knows if Mr Yeltsin will leave the ancient olive trees unpruned and majestic, if he will commit to the considerable expense of maintaining the rocket shapes of the cypresses. Only the services of the butler have been retained.

To survive, feuds require property, emotion and time to chew over the bitterness of things. When there is no one left to forgive, the feud is at an end. Then it is easy to forget.

October 16, 1997

THE EDGE OF VIABLE

Every year about this time I get dressed up as though I had a job like Nicola Horlick's. My husband puts on his Harris tweed suit, and we drive into Bury St Edmunds. It's the beginning of the sugar-beet season and there's nothing like sitting behind a convoy of sugar-beet lorries to inspire a little light conversation. 'What it boils down to is this,' I begin. 'What do we really want in life?'

My husband calls this my 'purposeful voice', a pitch that is not always welcome in the confined space of a Volvo travelling at 30 miles an hour. We are both nervous. We are on our way to a meeting with David Unwin, our farm accountant, and Jim Wilson, a cheerful but pragmatic Scotsman who is our farm adviser.

In my husband's file, a frayed brown crocodile folder with his father's initials, are all the figures: cash flow, budgets, yields and forecasts. Wheat down from £130 a tonne to £85. No premiums for malting barley. Sugar-beet prices dropping from £35 to £32 a tonne.

My see-through folder is the Optimist's file: letters announcing the farm has won Suffolk's 'Silver Lapwing' award for conservation in farming, and the Bale award for successful farm diversification. I've even photocopied a page from the 1998 *Good Food Guide,* with its democratic list of 'restaurants of the year'. Our vineyard café appears on the same page as the Connaught.

But I know that David and Jim are not interested in blue ribbons and silver cups. Their eyes focus on dropping farm prices, rising interest rates on farm overdrafts and higher machinery repair bills. Our farm, 1,100 acres, is in a category that is now described as 'the very edge of viable'.

There are few options facing farms like ours, with 850 acres under the plough. If one of us – my husband or I – worked full-time on the farm, ploughing, drilling, spraying, doing all the selling and buying – it would work. But neither of us can do that.

Our next possibility is to expand the work of the farm by taking on another 400 to 500 acres on contract. But those acres are not available to us.

That leaves us the final option: contracting out, having our fields farmed by either a large company or farmed by another local farmer who is in the same position we are in.

This is not just our story: it is the story of farmers all over the country. Pressure on farm incomes intensifies with every bank statement. Since 1992, 28,000 agricultural jobs have been lost. For three years now, Jim Wilson has been gently advising us to contract out.

Jim warns us that the next CAP reform will see a big fall in farm numbers, with a rapid swing to large, sophisticated, technical units. The present economics of grain and cropping will not improve and only the top 30% of farmers will remain profitable. These growers will be managing 80% of available land resources.

Continue farming Wyken ourselves, with two full-time men, and our farm income will not support our family. Contract out and we can go skiing at Easter, have a winter holiday, spend two weeks somewhere each summer.

It's hard to explain that the sight of one of our John Deere tractors drilling a field, seagulls chasing behind, moves me more than a Tuscan sunset. I have believed with all my heart that if a company that does not love the land can make a profit here, so can we.

Jim reminds me that we would not be selling our land, merely permitting skilled professionals to farm it. He does not know that for me the saddest line of all literature is the opening sentence of Isak Dinesen's autobiography: 'I had a farm...'

DARK BRAHMA LOVE

ALTHOUGH my mother stayed married to my father until the day she died, she tended to fall in love every ten years. This rocky rhythm of deep passion was hard on her daughters and wearing for her husband. It was also vexing to her own mother who mourned that 'Mary Alva has a heart like a hotel.'

It wasn't that she didn't love my father; she adored him and they stayed together throughout and despite my mother's emotional excursions. But Mama needed to be in love the way some women need to fix up houses or create gardens.

The effect this had on me was twofold: it made me wary of marriage and it instilled in me notions of loyalty and faithfulness beyond my years. Not for me the gypsy passions, the readiness to rush off.

Or so I thought. Now I am reaching the age when Mama began to slow down. She called it 'the Age of Memory and Remorse'. But I'm just beginning to feel the power of new love, the signs of a faithless heart.

For some years now, I have been the devoted and proud lover of that majestic creature, the bird of Hera: the peacock. My romance began with Phoebe and Oscar, bestowed on me by a local tapestrymaker. Within days of their arrival, Phoebe produced five buff-coloured eggs. A month later I had five little peabiddies. Peacocks are not known for their paternal temperament, so I scooted Oscar out of the nursery when his offspring were a few hours old.

In fact, Oscar was devoted. He stayed loyally beside Phoebe, separated by their prison wall of wire, throughout the infancy of the peabiddies. When the whole family was free, Oscar would ascend the tallest chimney on the house only after his wife and babies were safely installed on the roof ridge below. Two years later, when Phoebe was killed by a fox while sitting on her third brood, Oscar went into mourning from which he has never fully emerged.

Meanwhile, I have loyally defended this growing family against a gardener who does not appreciate the beauty of Oscar, who remains indifferent to the subtle refinement of the hens. Diligently, I've mastered the melancholy two-syllable language of the peacocks, my most convincing linguistic achievement. Friends who describe this as hysterical shrieking no longer appear in the visitors' book. And if I have regretted my peafowls' fondness for baby delphiniums, I have willingly accepted that *fraises des bois* are a legitimate part of their pay-packet.

But all that was before the arrival of the Dark Brahmas.

As is the trend these days, my love for the genuine aristocrat – the peacock, king of birds – has been supplanted by a passion for a mere commoner: a farmyard chicken, albeit a pure breed of great beauty and feathered feet. My Dark Brahmas, dressed in Chanel black and white with red accessories, originate, like the peafowl, from India. But unlike the peafowl, who nonchalantly accept me as a provider of turkey pellets, cracked corn and warm basmati rice, my Brahmas positively love my company. They rush to tell me their news and welcome my presence in the hen-house. They understand the art of gratitude and spend long hours in my lap being stroked like cats. My lap-chickens know their names: Sissy, Bessie, Lulu and Flo. Their consort, Rufus, is as handsome as Gary Cooper in *High Noon*, courteous, patient, strong.

My husband views my perfidious heart with alarm. He says the peafowl look forlorn. When I tell him that having an evening glass of wine in the hen-house with Rufus and the girls answers a deep need inside me, I see a sad look on his face. But I am in love and years away from Memory and Remorse.

November 13, 1997

V
Dormancy

THE SABBATICAL YEAR

COMING to terms with the finite number of lives you can reasonably pack into one life-span is a true sign of being a grown-up. You can watch *ER* and know that, even with enormous changes at the last minute, you will not be a doctor. All the jetés round the dining-room to Aaron Copland's *Rodeo* will not end with thunderous applause and a bouquet of roses.

Some days a single word can trigger wistfulness in me, my nostalgia for the lives I could have had. One such word is sabbatical, a tapestry of syllables that speaks of holy and scholarly lives that might have been mine. True, the appeal of a holy life was mainly sartorial. A year in a Catholic kindergarten left me besotted with the idea of being a nun. Not the modern Bride of Christ dressed in wraparound skirts and sandals, but a *Sound of Music* nun in acres of black cloth.

It was only slightly more likely that I might receive my sabbatical as a reward for scholarly endeavour. Although

I lectured cheerfully on such poets as Sylvia Plath, Robert Lowell, John Berryman and Philip Larkin to French university students, I never stayed in one place long enough to merit the gift of paid time, time to reflect, to clear away the clutter.

For a farmer, the Sabbatical Year described in the Bible, Leviticus 25, has great appeal: that every seventh year the land is to be left uncultivated: 'Thou shalt neither sow thy field nor prune thy vineyard.' In the Sabbatical Year, all debts are annulled.

Our Barclays Bank takes a dim view of the Old Testament Sabbatical Year, but I see the merits. Instead of the futility of set-aside, farmers could take a year when most of their fields would lie fallow, a time when the land could be nourished intelligently, not in the crass way tonnes of pig muck are spread on hot, airless days, but coherently returning organic waste to the soil at the right time in the right place, a year to remember that the strength of the earth is in the soil.

How I'd love a sabbatical for housebuilders who stick up identikit housing estates along the roundabouts in the countryside, a period when architects and builders would be required to live in those houses, reflect and learn.

I yearn for a Christmas sabbatical, a year when Father Christmas and all those elves could spend 12 months reading, walking and watching old movies instead of producing toys that say, 'Made in China'. Trees would be allowed during the Christmas sabbatical, but no new decorations, and all the presents would come from your own existing supply of stuff. A sabbatical on politics would have universal appeal. Politicians would spend the year working in schools, hospitals and small businesses in their constituencies. They would not be permitted a single public utterance. We could all bask in the tranquillity of ignorance and quiet. It would be like a timeless parliamentary recess, with *Yesterday In Parliament* replaced by letters and diaries, reflections on gardening, Alan Bennett reading *Winnie the Pooh*. The nation's morale would soar.

Finally, I think the perfect golden anniversary present for the Queen would be a sabbatical year, a time in which she could recharge her batteries, reflect on her life and times, and prepare for the years ahead. She and Prince Philip could go fishing in Alaska with William and Harry. They could stay in *Relais et Châteaux* in France, and have afternoon naps at Balmoral. The press would be absolutely forbidden to publish a photograph or report on any of their activities for the sabbatical year. Meanwhile, Prince Charles could run the show, and if all went well, he might get a sabbatical year when the Queen returned home.

November 20, 1997

FOR THIS GOOD LIFE

WE started reading *Little House on the Prairie* back in August, a chapter each evening sitting in the kitchen. I liked the idea of the family gathered round the table listening to the first-hand account of American pioneer life. My husband read and I provided the tunes for the snatches of songs: *'Old Dan Tucker went to town, Riding a mule, leading a hound.'*

When Sam squirmed I kicked him under the table. This usually happened during the passages which described how each thing was made. It took eight pages to make two stout doors and when the doors were finally hanging on their hinges there was the problem of keeping them shut. 'This was the way he made the latch: first he hewed a short, thick piece of oak...' and Sam would get this dozy look. He's the kind of boy who'd rather make a latch than listen to a description of how one is made.

In September Sam went off to prep school as a weekly boarder, but we persevered. Actually, the story didn't seem to suffer when reduced to Sunday night instalments, even when Indians were on the warpath and wolves were howling outside the little house on the Kansas prairie. Still, I was determined to get to the end of the story by Thanksgiving. I thought that three chapters in a row of American pioneer life would give Sam a feeling for his roots. Well, half his roots.

Also I was beginning to feel a little edgy. Reading together as a family made me feel like a Good Mother; taking four months to get to page 335 made me feel like I'd get the Bad Mama prize after all. Sam likes it that I grew up with Indians. He knows that the English colonists – his ancestors – thought the Indians were 'red men' because of the red-dyed bear grease they smeared on their skin to protect themselves from the mosquitoes that carried malaria. I don't have the heart to tell him that the Choctaw Indians I knew lived on reservations and I only saw them on Saturdays when they sat motionless outside the courthouse selling baskets. I haven't told him that the only howling of wolves I've heard is a cassette I bought at the Nature Store at the mall.

But a few hours before we were due to sit down to our Thanksgiving dinner, we read the next to last chapter, an elegiac passage about planting a garden full of sweet potatoes, cabbages, beans, peas and sweetcorn. The little sisters in the book tend the garden patiently and lovingly as they dream of their harvest. And then comes the terrible revelation: due to government stupidity they have built their log house and planted their crops three miles inside Indian Territory. On page 316 we learn that they have to pack up everything that will fit into their wagon and leave.

I was heartbroken. All their hard work for nothing. But their pa took it with all the fortitude and optimism of a pioneer. 'Never mind,' Pa says as they make camp on the first night of their new journey. 'We'll make a better garden. Anyway, we're taking more out of Indian Territory than we took in. Why, we've got a mule now.'

Tearfully, I tell Sam that we will begin the next volume, *Farmer Boy*, at Christmas. Sam says he reckons that by the time we finish all nine books he will be old enough to watch the video of *The Last of the Mohicans* (rated '15').

Meanwhile, we sit down to free-range turkey pan-smoked over grape vines, cornbread dressing and sweet potato pie in our big house on the Suffolk prairie. This food is my ministry. I tell Sam that we are eating all this because I want him to have his bearings, that knowing where you come from is part of feeling at home in the world. And then we say the blessing from Garrison Keillor so beloved by my pa: *Thank you, God, for this good life, and forgive us if we do not love it enough.*

December 11, 1997

RITUALS

MY sister loves to get married at Christmas. She married Brother on December 26 in a candlelit ceremony with eight bridesmaids dressed in cranberry red velvet. On top of the five-tier wedding cake was a bouquet of marzipan mistletoe.

When that marriage didn't work out, she used the wedding album as kindling at a family barbecue. After we had roasted hot dogs and marshmallows over the flames, she confessed the heat source. My Aunt Edna said it was a shame, because it had been a beautiful wedding and the photographer had come all the way from Memphis. Aunt Blanche was mad because she believes that chemicals in the leather, glue and photographs become carcinogenic when they reach a certain temperature.

But after a respectful interval, my sister got married again. This time it was what the papers call 'quietly' and there were no attendants, just family. It took place early in the afternoon of Christmas Eve and the wedding cake had white Christmas roses made of icing sugar.

My sister didn't ask for my advice on either of these occasions. In my experience, sisters don't have conversations like Lizzie and Jane in *Pride and Prejudice.* But I would have told her that Christmas was complicated enough without getting married as well. Everyone is already jumpy about money and presents and decorations and the long siege of togetherness and food that lies ahead, without adding wedding nerves.

And nowadays she might be told that marrying on Jesus's birthday is ritual overload. Rituals are a big topic and psychologists, theologians and anthropologists are all writing books about the importance of rituals in our lives. Not just the big, significant ones such as weddings, christenings, anniversaries and funerals, but new rituals: celebrations of solitude, ceremonies for healing wounds suffered in personal conflict – what we used to call making up.

I'm a great lover of rituals. I believe they give structure to life. I also think it is healthy to accept that some have a finite lifespan. This may be the last year that we leave Father Christmas a glass of early landed cognac from the Wine Society and a slice of fruit cake, together with organic carrots for the reindeer. That will be sad, although frankly I am ready to draw the line at the trail of his sooty footprints from the chimney right up the stairs.

We will still light the candles on our tree in the woods, but our Literary Christmas at the barn is now arranged every other year. This is a memorable evening when actors and writers read from contemporary Christmas writings - Laurie Lee, Truman Capote, Alastair Cooke, but no Charles Dickens – with the proceeds going to Shelter for Christmas. But in order for me to love this ritual, I can't do it every year. Otherwise it becomes just more hard work.

The truth is, we need our rituals spaced out, so that they are welcome rather than overwhelming. We need them simplified so they don't wear us out. And we need compromise rituals: I surrender Jane Grigson's frozen lemon soufflé for Delia's Christmas pudding, but we don't sit down to eat until after the Queen's speech.

There is another little ceremony that I relish on Christmas Day. First thing in the morning I put on my holiday apron, made for me by my sister to be worn during the long day's cooking. Meticulously embroidered with green silk thread, it reads 'The Christmas Martyr'. Wearing it helps me to remember that the happiness of all who are gathered together depends on the cook's good humour. My Christmas apron is made of recycled velvet in a shade of truly festive cranberry red.

December 4, 1997

BELIEVE

SOME people latch onto an idea and carry it round with them all their lives. For my friend Annie it is Christmas. She starts her Christmas shopping in January at the sales and it doesn't matter where she goes during the year – Venice, Papua New Guinea, Russia – she cuts short the history and culture and goes in search of figures for her crèche, ornaments for her tree and miniature treasures for the stockings. The china bowls in her house are filled year round with a potpourri called the Smell of Christmas. She has tea towels, canvas bags and oven gloves stencilled with angels, the plea 'BELIEVE' printed over the wings.

I admire Annie's passion. Instead of keeping a diary she has a red leather journal where she writes her Christmas list in all-consuming detail. My own lists are composed on the backs of used envelopes, which is not to say that I don't BELIEVE but simply that Christmas is not the main thing I have latched onto in life.

For a long time my cause was Justice. There was no

250

risk I deemed too sticky, no sacrifice too great, to slow down my pursuit of a more just world. I cast a cloud of gloom on many Christmas dinners by moping about the poor, the hungry, the sick and the weary who were not sharing our Christmas goose. My family was grateful that I turned a blind eye to goose justice.

But now I feel that the idea I carry around is more subdued. What I dwell on is loss. When loss – and its twin, a yearning for what is gone or out of reach – is what you have latched onto, Christmas is your season.

As we decorate our tree, I tell Sam about my special collection of white doves, with their brown glass eyes, real white (chicken) feathers and wiry feet that wound round the branches of my childhood Christmas trees. On one of my many moves, the box holding the doves was the one that got lost in shipping. 'You tell us this story every year,' says Sam as he helps his father untangle the lights.

With *Once in Royal David's City* in the background, I warm to the theme of loss. I think of the two short stories that Garrison Keillor lost when he left his briefcase behind in the men's room in the Portland train station, stories that in their disappearance have grown into landmarks of comic prose. I think of the emerald engagement ring that a friend's mother slipped from her finger and dropped into the sea when her husband announced that he no longer loved her, a ring that had survived three generations of married love lost for ever on an ocean bed.

Then I bring the theme of loss closer to home. This will be my first Christmas that didn't begin with a letter in October asking: 'What do you want more than you need?' My first Christmas without a book under the tree with a tag that says: 'If you read just one book this year...' This will be my first Christmas without parents.

After my mother died, my father began to spend Christmas here at Wyken. Last year he arrived with his suitcase filled with pecans, his own supply of Jack Daniels and thick, warm treasures from the L. L. Bean catalogue, his preferred source for Christmas shopping. With his white hair and large frame he looked like Father Christmas, but the real presents he brought to us were sanity, calm, patience, a loving irreverence and the most wonderful present of all – one I took so utterly for granted – the privilege of being a daughter.

A few weeks after my father returned home last year, a package arrived in a lumpy envelope. On the note inside was written: 'Consider this a late Christmas present. It's good to think from time to time about what is gone or out of reach. But don't dote on it. Love from Pa.' And there, a wiry foot poking through the bubble paper, was a single white dove.

December 18/25, 1997

HOME AWAY

HALF his life ago, when he was just over four years old, Sam asked if he could roast marshmallows in the hall. As it was the middle of the day and no fire was blazing, I said no. This refusal led to skilled negotiation followed by pleading, and ending with a tearful rebuke: 'You've ruined my life.'

Even to his volatile mama this was pretty dramatic stuff but I caught the ball before he made it to first base: 'Honey, I haven't begun to ruin your life. I will ruin it – that's my job – but I haven't even got started.' He seemed calmly to accept this dire prediction of his prospects. A day or so later when I heard the 'ruined my life' phrase on his favourite Robin Hood video I was dizzy with relief.

His dramatic utterance has stayed in my mind throughout the second half of his life. One red flag moment occurred ten minutes after a seven-hour drive to Cornwall, when he had an accident on a trampoline. Howling with pain, he swore that he had heard the bone

253

crack and his leg was broken ('I promise with all my heart,' he cried) but his father, behaving like a newly converted Christian Scientist, assured him that his leg would be fine in the morning. Eight weeks in a cast gave Sam plenty of time to wonder why his parents hadn't believed him.

Still, it wasn't until we loaded the car early in September and drove 40 miles to the prep school we had chosen for Sam, that I believed we might be on the approach road to ruin. For the first time in his life I was going against my maternal instinct, my common sense, my intellectual understanding, my heart. I was willingly giving up my full-time mother job and going part time, clocking in weekends and holidays but saying goodbye to the days of being the ubiquitous influence in his life.

Of course, weekly boarding means that Sam was not surrendered in the way his father and his father's father and his grandfather's father had been. As the proud mother of the goalie for the school's under nines 'A' team, every Wednesday I've made the two-hour round trip to watch Sam play football. On Saturdays, his father and I stand on wet and windy football pitches, nervous spectators who beam hysterical joy at each brilliant save, cringe when the rival team scores. We are getting used to our new positions on the sidelines of his life. As we eat egg sandwiches and drink tea with other parents while the boys have match tea, I calculate that we have 36 hours to be a family together before I bring him back early on Monday morning.

Perhaps I'm preoccupied with all this because Sam is home for the holidays. He has completed his first term at prep school, a small milestone in his life. Taller, thinner, he still wants me to read to him at night, to stay awhile after the light is out. But I'm no longer Maid Marion to his Robin Hood. He has joined the male world, switched his identification to his father. His godmother, Valerie, wise, alert and psychoanalytical, believes this is a triumph.

Now he knows things that I haven't taught him. He has fierce convictions that didn't come from me. And he is happy. When he tells me how much he loves playing squash, table tennis and indoor soccer in his free time, he is describing the dream of the only child: never being lonely.

There is a weird objectivity that comes when you no longer see your child daily. I look at Sam who now makes his bed and folds his clothes (mostly) and think that I understand why boarding schools continue to exist long after their colonial rationalisation has vanished. We believe that these schools will dilute our power in a positive way. We hope that, free from our constant gaze, our children will blossom. That in their post-childhood inventories, they won't believe we ruined their lives.

January 15, 1998

BIRTHDAY LETTERS

A MORNING to savour: husband off shooting, child at school. No one around to ask, 'Can I just have a word?' I grind pure Arabica beans for the luxury of real coffee and scan the Saturday papers. *Revealed: the most tragic literary love story of our time.* So my day explodes with a literary bombshell: after 35 years of silence, Poet Laureate Ted Hughes has written 88 poems that tell his side of his rocky marriage to the poet Sylvia Plath; powerful, sensitive, unsparing and unsentimental accounts of the exotic American girl who arrives in dreary postwar England to study at Cambridge on a Fulbright scholarship.

I discovered Sylvia Plath after her death, brooding during my second year at university over the angry, guttural, dangerous poems in *Ariel*. Ten years later came *Letters Home*, the claustrophobic letters which Sylvia wrote to her mother, missives full of straight-As and Plath's innocent faith in the Horatio Alger ethic: happiness is the right of everyone and is achieved through hard work; success is the reward for work. In 1975 such beliefs were deeply unfashionable but they struck a powerful chord in me.

As did all her writing about England. Through Sylvia Plath's sappy and dutiful letters, I got to know King's College chapel, the market-place in the square where she could buy leeks and books. I went to lectures, the Cambridge Labour Club dance, the Queen's opening of a veterinary lab at Newnham College ('she looked radiant in a Kelly-green princess-style coat and hat').

When Sylvia fell in love with Ted Hughes, so did I. Who could resist the handsome, brilliant Goliath, who loved poetry and food and wine? ('He stalked in with a packet of little pink shrimp and four fresh trout.') Only after I had lived in England for many years did I consider the cultural gaps between the Yorkshire countryman and the suburban American girl, canyons that might be minimised in academic settings, in cities. But with the birth of their first child, like a wicked stepmother came the familiar dream, the 'move to the country, escape the bad air and cramped spaces, raise children in nature' dream that led them to a thatched rectory in Devon.

In her pastoral idyll Sylvia made curtains, painted furniture, began riding lessons, kept bees, gave birth to their second child. And from there, Ted began the four-hour train journeys to London and the BBC that provided the work that paid the bills, journeys that would prove fatal to the marriage. I reckon this happens a thousand times a year. The difference is, this was a marriage of poets: a Poet Laureate to-be and his wife, an 'emotional terrorist'. Her journals and poems reveal a vulnerable, neurotic, jealous genius.

If she had survived, Sylvia Plath would now be 66 and probably a manic-depressive. But when her marriage failed, she was a little-known writer, a single mother living in the country, isolated from interesting friends, films, good libraries, exhibitions. Rural isolation can throw even the emotionally safe over the edge.

She managed to move to London for the last two months of her life, but by then the pessimism borne of the isolation of country life had gone too deep. Even her new town wardrobe from the Jaeger shop in Exeter could not disguise or heal her desolation.

Did she really mean to die when she put out the milk and biscuits for her children? What if she had stayed in London where playschools, doctors, editors and friends compensate for poisoned fumes and cramped spaces?

I bade farewell to Sylvia Plath when I surrendered the notion that great art requires great suffering. Maybe I just concluded that life is richer than death or art. But in retrospect I have come to believe that for the lonely, the depressed, for women on their own with small children, the country is not the place to be.

January 29, 1998

MARRIAGE WEEK

IT'S National Marriage Week and my friend Claire is spending it here at Wyken. She's welcome company because she's content to spend hours in the vineyard with me as I prune the vines. I explain to her that the cane closest to last year's now-mature wood will be the most fruitful, that the pruner counts two buds up from the root of that cane, allowing a finger's width beyond and cuts. But Claire, a skilled pruner of roses, prefers the 'pulling through', so we work as a team: I prune, she unravels the tangled prunings from the vines.

It's National Marriage Week and pruning is meditative work. Claire is reflecting on marriage. Rather, she is standing on a cold, south-facing slope trying to figure out why her children do not wish to get married.

Her son Angus, now 32 and a successful television producer, and their daughter-but-not-in-law, presented Claire and Hugh with their first grandchild two years ago. Maria, a willowy portrait painter with a distinguished client list, is pregnant again. Still no wedding bells.

'And now Charlie,' Claire moans. Younger daughter Charlotte read Classics at Cambridge, works on a national newspaper and lives with Theo, a junior doctor at St Thomas's. Their baby is due in September.

It's National Marriage Week and Claire, married 35 years to Hugh, wants to be the mother of a bride. Hugh blames his wife for the wayward genes. He could be right. Hugh, with his Norfolk estate, Mercedes 4x4, grandfather's Purdeys and tweed jackets, does not emerge as a man with bohemian tendencies. Claire, the daughter of an Eton housemaster, may have introduced strands of scholarship which, unchecked, could blossom into free-thinking.

Angus and Maria don't believe they should get married simply to please their parents. They insist they don't need legal or religious confirmation of their relationship. As for Charlie, she thinks marriage kills romance although she admits that children feel safer if their parents are married. And then there is the question of the estate: 3,000 acres, light land, no irrigation, a good shoot. Hugh knew that Angus wouldn't come back to Norfolk to farm and 'jolly good thing too. But I want him to enjoy this place and to take care of it.'

And that means to keep up the listed house, the flint estate cottages, the woods and the shoot, and to play a 'moral role' on the estate: attend church when you're home, not drive over the legal limit, and marry the mother of your children.

Hugh also refuses to allow the word 'partner' to be used in his presence. Claire's mother-in-law, a glamourous and enlightened dowager, uses the term 'comrade', etymologically accurate because it derives from the Latin *camera* for 'chamber'. Ma-in-law also claims that she is bored to death with unmarried people talking all the time about 'not needing a piece of paper to love each other'. She's got a point.

It's National Marriage Week and Hugh is meeting with his accountant and solicitors to try and tackle estate planning that prefers legal relationships to the more variable dictates of the heart. The solicitor points out that divorce wreaks more havoc with estate planning than not marrying at all. Claire pleads with me to conjure up the words that will persuade her children to make vows.

Pruning, like marriage, is an act of faith. Both thrive on a blend of rote and concentration. Both bring a sense of order to the landscape. I look with pride at the rows of trimmed, lissom vines, and I feel contentment in my marriage. But even I cannot give a set of clear, sequential, compelling reasons why anyone should plant vines in Suffolk or get married.

February 19, 1998

BINGO!

WHEN I was growing up, housekeepers lived in literature. The only one I knew in real life worked for a patrician lawyer whose wife had died young, leaving him with a daughter who had multiple sclerosis. Georgia cooked, cleaned, nursed, sang, washed, mended and listened.

It struck me as important that Georgia was never called a cook or a maid, but a 'housekeeper', a title that signified honour and authority. Years later when I first came to Wyken, I was introduced to the housekeeper. Although she lived in the village, only worked mornings and came to work on a Vespa, Jean had authority. She also had memory. She could describe the handsome Frank Heilgers, my husband's cousin, who bought the estate in 1920 and who, as MP for Bury St Edmunds, had presented her with the silver cup on prize day in the village school. That was in 1937 when she was thirteen. At fourteen, Jean left school to begin work as a parlourmaid at Garboldisham Manor.

Except for five years during the Second World War, when she worked in London, Jean has spent her whole life in this corner of Suffolk. When Stan Woodrow, a village boy who'd spent the war with the RAF in Egypt was demobbed in 1947, they married and settled here.

Jean began working at Wyken in the 1950s, when my husband's grandparents inherited the estate. In those days she fitted her hours round the school day, but when her third son was born, she gave up working. She came back here after my parents-in-law took over. When I arrived, there was also a cook, a 'servants sitting room' and a kitchen where food was cooked but not eaten.

In the first years of my marriage, Jean was a valued newfound friend. She relished the changes that were going on and she never complained about the mess and chaos. On shoot days, we slaved away together, me cooking, Jean setting up the drinks in the hall and the dining room. After lunch, when the guns departed, we collapsed in the kitchen over banoffi pie and sloe gin.

In late January, we would go off to Bury St Edmunds for shopping and lunch. One year I booked a table at the town's landmark Angel Hotel, where we were the only two people sitting in the elegant dining room. As we sipped our glasses of Gewürztraminer, Jean whispered, 'I haven't been here since I was two weeks old'. She then explained that the Angel was where she had been 'handed over' to the woman who Jean would call Mum all her life.

Jean, slender and girlish, spends her afternoons working in her garden. Until a few years ago she was active in the Red Cross, the Mothers' Union and the Poppy Appeal. Each autumn she takes a coach trip with her sister-in-law, usually to Scotland. Once a month she and Stan go to the Theatre Royal in Bury for an evening of country music. On Saturday nights they play bingo in Thetford, splitting their winnings fifty-fifty. In April we had a party at Wyken to celebrate their 50th wedding anniversary.

And then last Saturday night Stan won the National Bingo: £106,000. On Monday Jean came to work with a grin and a giggle.

When people as good, modest, honourable and hard-working as Jean and Stan win like that, you begin to think there is a God of Small Things. You also start thinking selfishly about yourself: 'I reckon this means you will stop work.' 'Oh no,' she replied. 'But if you can manage, I wouldn't mind going from three mornings to two.'

Tomorrow, when Stan brings Jean to work, he'll be driving their brand-new, midnight-blue ford fiesta from Fordham's in Ixworth. We will all be outside waiting.

February 26, 1998

264

FARM SALE

IN the movie of this day I'd like to be played by Meg Ryan. The cameras would start to roll as soon as you come off the A143 onto the Walsham road, a lonely banjo accompanying the convoy of Land Rovers across a farmscape so flat it looks as if Columbus was right all along.

You know you've crossed onto our land when the mooniness of the arable landscape gives way to green: copses of trees, woodland, sprawling hedges lining the road and, in the middle of a field, a dilapidated barn straight out of John Steinbeck. The farm vehicles turn into a meadow that is filled with agricultural archaeology: Smythe drills, ploughs, a stack of feed sacks that read Wyken Hall Farm.

The bright sun warms the men who gather round the catering van, eating bacon sandwiches, drinking coffee out of styrofoam cups. Another group waits to register outside the new Portakabin, under the sign, 'Clarke &

Simpson, Chartered Surveyors'. My husband, courteous, shy, with eyes as blue as Anthony Hopkins's, shakes hands with men in flat caps who remember his father, his grandfather.

But this is not a film. This is a farm sale. It's not a tale of farm depression, rural destitution and bankruptcy, although in this insular rural community there is the unshakeable feeling that catastrophe looms. In the language of auctioneers, this is a sale of 'agricultural machinery and effects'. It is also the end of an era. We are not selling the land but we are selling what it takes to farm it: three John Deere tractors; a New Holland combine that has seen only two harvests; ploughs; sprayers; a drill so new that you could eat your dinner off it.

No casting director could find the extras who come to farm sales, men born to farming whose faces are marked by a hundred seasons, men who remember the old Boby seed dresser and the blacksmith's bellows, men who have lived through the swift turning of this century and still believe the land is God.

This isn't the stuff of movies but I feel as if I am watching a film. I cannot believe that this is our farm, the contents of our barns, a farm history that dates from Domesday, spread out in 330 lots. Leaning against my husband, I listen to the auctioneer speaking the rapid, unintelligible language of the farm auction. Chris Clarke, more handsome than Jeremy Irons, as civilised as an

Oxford don, knows the value of every lot, the meaning in each slight movement.

For a time we are joined by Robert Claydon. After today, he will be farming Wyken. We were never interested in an agribusiness. Claydons have farmed in Suffolk for 100 years and Robert is a good farmer who cares about the ecology as well as the economics of farming.

I try not to stare as I look at the faces of our farm men. They both came to Wyken straight from college. Neil, our tractor driver, will stay, but John, our farm manager who's been here 17 years, will move on. Farming is all he has ever cared about. Now he wonders if there's a future in it.

My husband carefully notes the final price of each bid. He believes that what we are doing is best for the long-term future of the estate. I fight back tears as my three John Deeres go, all bought by a Frenchman based in Lincolnshire. The combine fetches £54,000, but half of that will go towards our final payment on it.

This won't be a film because there isn't a bad guy. The enemy is a belief: get big or get out. In movie talk that's too reflective, too vague. And even with Meg Ryan and banjos, you need a truly happy ending.

March 5, 1998

267

FALL FROM GRACE

'I used to think if you fell from grace it was more likely than not the result of one stupendous error, or else an unfortunate accident. I hadn't learned that it can happen so gradually you don't lose your stomach or hurt yourself in the landing... I've found it takes at least two and generally three things to alter the course of a life. You slip around the truth once, and then again, and one more time, and there you are, feeling, for a moment, that it was sudden, your arrival at the bottom of the heap.'

I'VE been chewing over these thoughts that begin Jane Hamilton's novel *A Map of the World*, from my position on the football pitch at Sam's school. It's the last match of the season and my thoughts are elsewhere, on a man in his fifties, who was once a boy at this same school housed in a vast Victorian country house with its own observatory and acres of green playing-fields overlooking the River Orwell. As I shout 'well saved!' and 'tackle, tackle!' I wonder if he was happy here, a school where games matter so much. It can't have been easy for him, arriving after a year spent in bed with polio.

I remember being surprised to learn that Jonathan Aitken had gone to this modest prep school in Suffolk – not Summer Fields or the Dragon or Ludgrove. Then I learned that his father had been the Member of Parliament for Bury St Edmunds after the war, winning the same seat that my husband's cousin occupied until he died in a train crash travelling down to London in 1944.

Those two things – a prep school and a familiar parliamentary seat – are all I have in common with Jonathan Aitken. In all the years he was a colleague of my husband, I saw him only once, at a drinks party at No 12 Downing Street where he stood with his daughter, in a tall, visually idyllic *pas de deux*. They looked almost too good to talk to but I managed a few words because of a letter he wrote when my husband returned to the back benches, a letter of genuine eloquence and memorable kindness.

For some time now I've been trying to understand this man's fall from grace, this man who spent his so-called formative years where my son now spends his. Dimestore psychologists could find significance in a frail little boy being sent to boarding-school at all, especially to a place where the winds blow straight from Siberia. Another diagnostician might go back earlier, to the solitary years confined to bed. Consider: does survival of serious childhood illness give the victim delusions of invulnerability? And there's plenty of psychological meat in the apocryphal story of the rich, great uncle Max (Lord) Beaverbrook, telling the young Jonathan, by then in his first year at Eton, 'You are a very bright boy and I am going to pay you the greatest compliment: I am not going to leave you a cent.' The inheritance of great wealth is a certain curse but only the most robust will be undamaged as the (relatively) poor relation surrounded by unattainable splendour.

But the truth is, even after hours of idle speculation, I just don't get it. I cannot accept the verdict that Jonathan Aitken's fall from grace is the result of a 'silly lie'. I'm stuck with the belief that you slip around the truth, once, then again, and each time the edges blur still further, until there is a lifetime accumulation of risk, deals and reckless versions of the truth. The schizophrenia begins to fit as well as a Saville Row suit – I think about Aitken's hero Richard Nixon (was that a sign?), about Kennedy, Alan Clark, Clinton – as principles become more and more disconnected from behaviour.

A cheer as Sam's team wins 3-0. As they race back for match tea, I search their flushed faces, looking for signs of outsized ambition, audacious virility, fortitude. These are their formative years and I'm no oracle but I whisper under my breath: 'Stick to the truth; that's old, but stick to it.'

April 9, 1998

BRER HARE

My grandmother believed some folks are born out of place. She always thought that's what happened to me. Seems like I came into this world with a feeling for Englishness. At a tender age I appreciated the difference between Brer Rabbit, who inhabited my birthplace, and Peter Rabbit. 'Skin me, Brer Fox,' sez Brer Rabbit, 'snatch out my eyeballs, t'ar out my ears by de roots, 'n cut off my legs, but do please, Brer Fox, don't fling me in dat briar patch.' Peter Rabbit, a very English rabbit, finding himself in a similar predicament, 'shed big tears, but his sobs were overheard by some friendly sparrows, who flew to him in great excitement, and implored him to exert himself.'

I reckon everybody knows that Brer Fox caught Brer Rabbit by the hind legs and slung him right in the middle of the briar patch. After he waited a few minutes he looked up the hill and saw Brer Rabbit sitting cross-legged on a chinkapin log, hollering: 'Bred 'n bawn in a briar patch, Brer Fox – I'se bred 'n bawn in a briar patch!'

Of course, the difference between Peter Rabbit and Brer Rabbit is not merely cultural. Peter Rabbit is a short, nervous, little English rabbit who makes life hard for his mother, a stressed single parent. But Brer Rabbit, independent, clever, intrepid, isn't a rabbit at all but a Jack Rabbit, which is the common name for hares in America. Just look at the illustrations of Brer Rabbit by A. B. Frost and you will see the long hind legs and powerful loins which account for the hare's exceptional speed.

The brown hare has much longer ears than the rabbit. And hares have big hearts, weighing from 1 to 1.8% of the total body weight of the hare. A rabbit's heart weighs only 0.30% of its body weight, making rabbits closer to squirrels with 0.60%. Big hearts mean greater endurance.

Naturally, Beatrix Potter preferred rabbits because they are nuclear family creatures. The babies are born pink and naked and cuddle with their mama in a warm, cosy place that has every comfort. The breakfast dishes are Blue Italian Spode and William Morris curtains hang in the rabbit hole.

The hare is a different story. Born fully dressed, with sharp eyes (gamekeepers claim they are blue) and ears as finely tuned as a poet's, the hare begins his life of solitude soon after he is born.

In our household we may shoot rabbits but the hare is sacred. In spring we spend hours walking in the fields, solemnly watching the March dances of the athletic hares as they leap through the newly drilled fields like Russian ballet dancers. We called our vineyard restaurant the Leaping Hare in honour of the magical creatures that occupy this farm in great numbers. A 1935 wood engraving of a leaping hare by Clare Leighton graces our wine label. Hares in clay, porcelain and bronze fill our house. Jugged hare never appears on the menu.

During the late 1980s when hares began dying at Wyken, I sent hare carcasses by Red Star to the Cambridge University veterinary unit for pathology reports at £35 a go. The eventual diagnosis: Brown Hare Syndrome, a virus blamed on the stress of overpopulation. It seems to have disappeared. Now, when I do combine duty during harvest, I'm mesmerised by the chorus line of hares.

There is only one hare that troubles me: the Easter Hare. Our larder is filled with chocolate hares and creme eggs he's left behind. I have never known how this hare gets here or why he hides the eggs that we dyed the day before. My ambivalence about this creature may call into question other miracles such as tooth fairies and reindeer on rooftops. The problem is, I believe that leaving a trail of Cadbury's mini eggs in the herb garden is really a bunny thing. Any self-respecting Jack Rabbit would rather be flung in a briar patch.

April 16, 1998

273

FUNERAL PLANS

'I DON'T want a memorial service,' says my fellow guest over breakfast. 'I'd prefer a rather grand funeral,' he adds, arranging his gently scrambled eggs onto their platform of fried bread.

We are a large and amiable house party, sitting round an oval table in a dining room with long windows that look over an estuary that leads to a river that leads to the ocean that leads to America. It is a setting of such perfection that funeral versus memorial service seems out of place, but we are inspired by the Sunday papers and their reports of the funeral of David Hicks, who was buried the day before.

Hicks planned his funeral as meticulously as he did the houses and gardens that made his reputation in life. He designed his coffin – sycamore, painted grey – and asked his gardeners and the warden, clerks and beadle of the Salters' Company to be his pallbearers. Instead of the plastic green grass that surrounds coffins on their journeys from church to churchyard, he insisted on ivy. There was no black hearse leading the cortège, but a stately Range Rover bearing a flag with his coat of arms.

Over the breakfast table we are united in the wish not to have Canon Henry Scott Holland's poetic admonition that we are only in the next room. What brought a tear to the eye on first hearing has become like a ghastly ghostly greeting card for the bereaved.

Still, we are sharply divided between those who believe elaborate funeral instructions are a burden to widows, widowers and children, and those who feel it is deliverance to have all the decisions made. As we drink cups of strong coffee the mistress of the house reads aloud the final paragraph from *The Sunday Telegraph's* account of David Hicks's funeral. In it, Hicks's son, Ashley, describes his father's experience when he was 12: 'He was at Charterhouse and his headmaster called him into his office and said: 'Well, Hicks, your father has died but we think it's best if you don't go to the funeral.' He got home to find his brother dressed in his father's clothes, lying in his father's bed. His mother thought it would help him get over it.'

I never met David Hicks. I've seen rooms that he designed and photographs of his garden and I've always loved the immaculate exuberance, the beautiful precision. Even without the trauma of his father's death, I believe that he would have wanted to design an occasion as important as his farewell to all his earthly rooms.

'He was quite fortunate to have an illness that gave him time to prepare his final designs,' says my neighbour, but I demur. It's not a case of having the time so much as taking the time. Death is always there and preparing for it is as wise as planting avenues that you will never see touch the sky.

I'm on the side that believes that leaving behind a master drawing for the final ritual of your life is a wonderful gift for your family and friends. My own family is still stinging from a death a couple of months ago. Uncle Jimmy died of a heart attack at a church supper but the funeral had to be put off for ten days because his four children couldn't agree on whether to bury or to cremate. Before they got round to choosing the hymns, one cousin was consulting her astrologer and another cousin was consulting his lawyer. It was not the comforting ritual of farewell that everyone needed.

Unlike David Hicks, Uncle Jimmy probably would have settled for the least expense and trouble. But I believe that family and friends need a chance to reflect on the life that's ended. The living need small ceremonies. On the long drive from Cornwall to Suffolk I shall chew over revisions to my own instructions. I too dislike hired pallbearers and plastic grass.

April 23, 1998

THE MADONNA

ALTHOUGH it is one of those spring days when I require two sweaters and cashmere socks, Mr Reekie has come to open the swimming pool. The appointment was made two weeks ago when I was hot and sweaty from cleaning out the sheep pen and longed for a cooling swim. Now it is so windy and cold I can't even wander out to see how they are getting on.

I love swimming. I prefer water to land and I prefer oceans to pools. I don't really think of myself as the swimming-pool type. We don't actually call it 'the pool'. We call it 'the Madonna'. Art lovers and historians who knew the 15th-century painting of the Madonna and Child by the Master of the Bargello are frankly a little shocked that the serene and touching painting went to Christie's and in its place we have a swimming-pool.

Maybe the contrast between the rare and irreplaceable painting and the swimming-pool wouldn't be so glaring if we had built the kind of pool favoured by architects: black liners set in stone surrounds to look like ponds. My sister sent me a photograph of Martha Stewart's unheated (ecologically correct) swimming-pool. She claims that the dark, unpainted concrete helps to absorb the warmth of the sun and, in turn, warms the water. But despite all the aesthetic arguments, I couldn't make the swan dive of faith required to believe that dark English water would be warmer.

The truth is, we wouldn't have a swimming-pool at all if we hadn't had such a grand firm of London solicitors. Libel laws prevent me from revealing their hallowed names but you would recognise them immediately. The 'family solicitors' as long as anyone can remember, they advised us and organised all the papers when my mother-in-law gave us the Madonna as a wedding present, just as they did when my mother-in-law inherited the picture from her mother.

The painting of the chaste Madonna with her baby son was not a seamless acquisition. When we hung it above the drawing room fireplace our friend Lucilla, a distinguished picture restorer, was horrified: 'Smoke will do untold damage,' she warned. Others counselled against hanging it where it would be visible when the gardens were open. Natural light was taboo and insuring it for its true value was the equivalent of buying a new Volvo every year. I began chomping about staying in a house with something so valuable it was sensible for thieves to kill me for it. My mother-in-law, the least materialistic person I've ever known, hinted we were free to sell it.

It seems ungrateful to sell a wedding present, but a few years ago we decided that she would approve of the Madonna paying off the farm overdraft and contributing to the school fee mountain. Other projects danced in our heads: a pond with a thatched hut in the centre, a reservoir. Then we discovered a small problem, called 'exempted'. If my husband had been left the painting, we could have sold it at a friendly tax rate. Receiving it as a gift a few years earlier meant that we would pay tax of 80%. Keep the painting and you are exempted from paying tax; sell and you pay at the tax rate when it was first bequeathed. Complicated stuff and no one liked to murmur 'badly advised'.

The Madonna gazed shyly from the cover of the Christie's catalogue. The painting sold handsomely. I thought our proceeds of 20% would get lost in the farm borrowing and should go towards something pleasurable instead, hence the swimming-pool. The morals of this story are as obscure as unpainted concrete: treasures are better left than given; country solicitors are more solicitous than London solicitors; and, if you are thinking of building a pool, first read chapter VIII of Russell Page's *The Education of a Gardener.*

May 14, 1998

1968

I AM sitting on a bed of barley straw in the sheep pen with Belinda and her twin lambs. Beside me is a sheep first-aid kit that looks like a prop from M*A*S*H*, a pile of Saturday and Sunday papers and a tumbler of 1982 Langoa Barton miraculously left over from last night's dinner. I am here for the evening, bottle-feeding the lambs, injecting Belinda with antibiotics and thinking about 1968.

My thoughts were triggered by a call from a young journalist. She wasn't even born in 1968 but she's writing one of those 'where are they now' pieces. Someone suggested she get in touch with me for a telephone interview although, as she confessed, 'I'm not sure who you were in '68.' Unfortunately, I couldn't tell her. I'd just discovered one of my Shetland ewes with mastitis, an inflammation of the udder caused by infectious organisms which get in via the teat. By the time I noticed that half of her udder was red, hard and hot, the ewe was already in the acute stage. I was rushing off to the vet's to collect the antibiotic and steroid injections and special tubes to strip out the teat.

According to *The Veterinary Book for Sheep Farmers*, 'treatment of severe mastitis is very unrewarding in the majority of cases and should be aimed at saving the ewe's life, since it is rarely possible to save the udder'. I made the ewe as comfortable as possible with deep straw bedding and, a couple of hours after her first injections, brought her lambs inside to make her feel more at ease. I'm bottle-feeding so that they won't bother her.

According to the rules of common sense, it is also unrewarding to try and explain to anyone who you were in 1968. It's a long story and, looking through the weekend papers with photographs of a white-haired Tom Hayden at an Oscar party, Vaclav Havel behind a presidential desk and Jane Fonda, elegant and powerful on the arm of Ted Turner, it feels like reading about landmines in the pages of *Hello!*. It is hard to poke about in the serious history of your past and not wind up with a version that trivialises it.

What I should have told the journalist is that the Sixties and 1968 were not the same thing. That who I – or anyone – was 30 years ago doesn't matter as much as the events that made us think and do and feel things that were so radically different from what we had felt before. The year began with the trial of Dr Spock, charged with inciting young American men to resist the draft. In early April Martin Luther King was assassinated; in May nine million workers in France joined a general strike begun by students. In June Bobby Kennedy was shot. In August the Russians invaded Czechoslovakia. We wept as we read of Dubcek quoting the poet Hölderlin: 'And tenderly I pledged my heart to the grave and suffering land.'

Of course, what the journalist wants is a story: the 1968 activist who chanted 'All Property is Theft' now living on a country estate in Suffolk; the protester, on whose walls hung the *mai soixant-huit* poster 'Demand the Impossible' now surrounded by ancestral portraits. Maybe it is churlish of me not to comply. Perhaps, along with spell-check and reality-check, I need a humour-check.

The patient ewe's eyes thank me for looking after her babies. My hard-line comrades would say I am no longer a humanist but a sheepist. The truth is, no one can survive for ever at the fever pitch the terrible events of 1968 required. Life is a less dramatic hue. The war in Vietnam ended, thanks to the ground swell of opposition. The Cold War has subsided. Deep down I like to think my life never veers far from the principles of those years. That on my bed of straw I can relish the last swallow of the Langoa Barton while feeding a sweet and greedy lamb, that all my days I will 'Demand the Impossible'.

May 21, 1998

ON YOUR FARM

WE served pan-fried quail, garlic grits, buttermilk biscuits and fig preserves and, despite the early hour, Wyken wine. We sat, not in front of the compulsory Aga, but in our newly converted 400-year-old barn, in the vineyard restaurant which is the heart of our farm diversification.

Taking part in *On Your Farm* was one of the big moments in my life. All those years of Sunday mornings in bed with my Fortnum & Mason Darjeeling, I listened to farmers and their hard-working, modest wives talking about the WI and death duties, milk fever and pulpy kidney. I never dreamt that someday I might be the farmer's wife, nervously accepting Oliver Walston's praise for my quail and explaining about grits. Unlike other farmers' wives, however, every time my farmer husband was in interesting mid-sentence, I'd butt in, ranting about set-aside and the Common Agricultural Policy, my voice rising above the authentic tinkling of knives and forks.

Those were the days. Now James Boyle has shortened *On Your Farm*, which chews away the leisurely feel of a Sunday breakfast. Worse still, he's moved it from the civilised time of 7:15am to the un-Sunday hour of 6:35am. It was completely by chance a few weeks ago that I heard the Duke and Duchess of Devonshire serving Oliver Walston a breakfast of oatcakes, wild boar sausage and Welsummer eggs, all from the Chatsworth Farm Shop.

I felt like I'd won the lottery. The Duchess is my heroine and mentor. She may be a mere duchess but she is the queen of farm diversification, developing it into a fine art and industry. I'll never forget the thrill of my first visit to Chatsworth. I bought for a godson a sweater knitted from the wool of her Jacob sheep, and copies of *Hons and Rebels* and *Love in a Cold Climate* from a table with a handwritten sign which said 'Family Books'. I suspect I saw paintings by Rubens and Poussin on that day but the only postcard I bought was of the dreamy portrait of Deborah, the present Duchess, by Annigoni.

The Duchess calls her Duke a 'town yob' because she is a true country woman. Like a born again Christian, she passionately evangelises on country matters. She also adores commerce and her Farm Shop employs 25 people full-time. Her presence at the Chelsea Flower Show is legendary, tirelessly pushing her garden furniture from Chatsworth Carpenters while other duchesses drink champagne in the President's tent.

This is the Mitford sister who used to sing 'Someday My Duke Will Come', and her Duke is everything a duke should be. He believes that landowners who fight access and the right to roam are intolerable, insisting 'they will lose in the end and therefore they should lose gracefully, willingly and at once – it's a question of goodwill.' He laments the ever-increasing divide between town and country, and worries about city people who want the countryside to become a theme park. 'The indigenous industries in the Peak District are quarries, but city folk don't want new quarries. Do away with quarries and you do away with jobs; do away with jobs and you do away with communities. It's that simple.'

His Duchess interrupts him in a pleasantly familiar way, bucking and snorting about threats to her unpasteurised English cheeses and beef on the bone. 'Before, we were paid for our bones. Now we pay £3,500 to a man to collect them. We are allowed to sell bones to dogs but only dogs who can sign the form.'

I worry that *On Your Farm* won't survive the likes of James Boyle, who is the greatest single contributor to the ever-increasing divide between town and country. And I worry that visionaries such as the Duchess are destined to become rare breeds. Sunday mornings and country life will never be the same.

May 28, 1998

THE WORLD OF INTERIORS

AFTER we had been married a year we finally reached the dining room. By then we had transformed most of the downstairs, turning the drawing room into the 'Women's Room', with a ceiling painted 'the soul of blue' and creamy yellow walls lined entirely with portraits of women, 14 in all, including a melancholy de Laszlo of my mother-in-law in her twenties, a pen-and-ink of Nancy Astor's sister by Charles Dana Gibson and a life-size panel of a Spanish señora by Vanessa Bell.

The latter was one of a group of pictures by Bell and Duncan Grant commissioned by Cunard for the *Queen Mary*. The paintings were all rejected, causing a grave rupture between the Bloomsbury set and my husband's grandmother, a friend and patron of the artists as well as wife of the chairman of John Brown, shipbuilders for Cunard. When my husband bought the picture some 40 years later he was unaware of its troubled provenance.

But if the drawing room had a feminine feel, the dining

room was stuck in the masculine time warp of a thousand English country house dining rooms: early hunting prints by Wolstenholme of the Essex, Badminton and Bexley Hunts. Underneath the long oak table, the turkey carpet lay with its threadbare perimeter marked by feet shuffling through a hundred years of five-course dinners, the centre a soft and fluffy sanctuary where no legs were long enough to reach. Dangling from the ceiling was a buzzer whose electronic whine summoned staff to take away, bring more, plenish and replenish.

Inspired by the date of the room (somewhere between 1570 and 1640) we asked a French artist living in Tunbridge Wells to paint a mural of the wildlife of Wyken growing – with Elizabethan abandon – off grapevines. Mr Lassalle, a purist who concocted his oil-based distemper and ground his own pigments, adhered religiously to historical techniques. He also kept Ramadam, which meant that he began work at dawn and ate only in the evening.

He created a wall of ecstatic flora and fauna in warm and natural colours, achieving the pinnacle of country-house ambition: it looks as though it has always been there. My husband secretly regrets the presence of French partridges with their telltale red legs instead of the rarer, timid English partridge, and the hares are hidden behind the refectory table – which Mr Lassalle, also an expert in early English oak, revealed to be Victorian and not the

Jacobean treasure we'd believed – but all in all our joy was great.

All this detail is fresh in my mind because I've just agreed to the interior of the house appearing in a magazine. I always vowed I never would, a somewhat hypocritical position as I adore gazing at pictures of other people's rooms and could pass an exam on the early issues of *The World of Interiors*. I cited privacy as the exalted reason for my regular refusals but the real reason behind my reluctance was the knowledge that I had lost interest in the Eighties Cult of the House.

Of course my anxiety was wholly unnecessary. Looking at the photographs no one would recognise our house. Mantelpieces and table tops are bursting with *objets*, flowers and books immaculately stacked. There is an all-pervasive feeling of richness and tranquillity, the orderly perfection of Dutch paintings. The jetsam and flotsam of real life – clothes, mugs, radiators, digital clocks, ganglia of wires dangling from sockets – have all been banished by the stylist's magic wand. In the slivers of text that will company these images, I suspect I will not be quoted as saying that the country fell apart in the late Eighties because everybody with a lick of sense became obsessed with fixing up their houses. These rooms are the soul of blue and everything that jars has been edited out.

June 4, 1998

VI
Renewal

FEVER PITCH

I've just won a £100 bet. Collecting it might be a problem because the loser is nine years old and it would wipe out his entire savings, including his stash of book tokens. Besides, making him pay might make him feel crummier than he already feels.

I'm not much of a betting woman. It happened like this.

Sam, opening his third pack of England World Cup Medals from Sainsbury's: 'Wow, another Paul Gascoigne. Now I've got a swap.'

Me: 'Maybe you'd better hang onto it. It could become really valuable, like Edward VIII coins.'

Sam: 'What do you mean?'

Me: 'I mean I don't think Paul Gascoigne will be playing in the World Cup.'

Sam: 'Are you crazy? Of course he'll play. I bet you £100 he plays.'

I don't know when I became so certain that Gascoigne

would not make it to France. It's not as if I spend my Mondays reading *Times Sport*. My knowledge of football is in the category of what the scientist Rupert Sheldrake defined as 'morphic resonance'. Sheldrake's theory is that knowledge is transmitted through invisible sound waves. One day a blue tit pecks through the silver foil top of the milk bottle and finds a delicious *petit déjeuner* of cream. Six months later, blue tits throughout the United Kingdom have learned via sound waves about this matinal feast.

Football has been like that. One day I'd never heard of Terry Venables, Glen Hoddle, Gazza, David Seaman, FA Cups, yellow cards, Alan Shearer, Liverpool, Paul Ince. Now I know defenders from forwards, can scan the midfield and agonise with the last line of defence: the goalkeeper. I talk about the traditional qualities of the English game – passion, pace and power – and the importance of holding onto the ball.

Maybe the acquisition of this knowledge hasn't been as seamless as it feels, but I can cite two defining moments. One was the semi-final during Euro '96, the first time I allowed Sam, then aged seven, to stay up and watch a football match late at night. The game ended in tears but we were both hysterical with excitement throughout.

The next big moment was last season when Sam was mascot for Ipswich Town. He's a member of the Ipswich Town Junior Blues and his name was pulled from the hat, but he felt as though he had just been recruited. Even his mother decided that the price of the goalie strip, hitherto described as rip-off materialism, was worth the investment as he led the team onto the pitch to the roar of 30,000 voices. He warmed up with the team, informing us later that 'real goals are bigger than churches'. Best of all, Ipswich beat Wolverhampton 3-0.

So what converted me? Well, I like the new and exuberant populism of football. I am delighted that the old ethos – that rugby was a working-class game played by gentlemen and football a gentleman's game played by the working class – is now as dead as the dodo. Like 'soccer moms' in America who have embraced the game because it isn't as brutal as American football, I prefer football to rugby because it requires speed and intelligence over brute strength and monster necks.

However it may seem to nine-year-olds, losing Gascoigne isn't a disaster. Mothers and coaches round the country are explaining that if you want to be a sportsman you have to look after your body, you can't eat kebabs in Soho at one o'clock in the morning, and you can't smoke 20 cigarettes a day and pull off the brilliant, unpredictable moves that made you famous. That, even if you have lavish talents, to be an outstanding player you need great discipline. I hope someone is talking to Gascoigne too. And in case they aren't, this one's for you, Gazza: it's never too late to grow up.

June 11, 1998

LLAMA JAMAS COME HOME

FORGIVE me if I indulge in a little wistfulness for the Eighties. Not a nostalgic longing for its excess and decadence, but for its entrepreneurial optimism. Everyone I knew was on the cusp of an idea that would lead to fame and fortune. My friend Kerry was poised to launch her mail-order catalogue of Forbes tartan products – baby blankets, picture frames, sponge bags – aimed at the Scottish American market. Her husband James, an Old Etonian and brilliant chef, already had the principal Eighties dream: a catering business that serviced film shoots.

Other friends saw their empires in hand-painted wine coasters, reproduction Edwardian light fittings, folding boats that fit on the roof of a car. My own plan was quintessential Eighties in the Country: llamas.

Not just llamas gazing through heavenly long eyelashes and tilting their graceful necks, but a family of llamas known as the Llama Jamas: Mama Llama Jama,

Papa Llama Jama, Lulu Llama Jama and Larry Llama Jama, characters in a limitless series of books. I managed to write the first three: Volume I when they go from Peru to the Napa Valley, Volume II, the Llama Jamas in Paris and Volume III, the Llama Jamas in London. My entrepreneurial dream did not stop with the books that owed a modest debt to Babar and Madeleine. The 'marketing arm' included children's sleepwear, aka Llamajamas, velvety soft jimjams in yummy llama colours of chocolate, coffee and vanilla. Each pair would come in a cuddly Llamajama sac which would also include a teeny weeny Llama Jama story.

My husband, not an Eighties man by nature, was persuaded to take out a copyright on the name Llama Jama. Farm buildings were considered as offices for the Llama Jama empire. I visited mills in Nottingham in my search for the perfect 100% cotton fabric. The manuscripts were sent to publishers and I waited for the Walt Disney Corporation to enter a bidding war.

Even now I'm a little sensitive when acquaintances ask 'Whatever happened to the Llama Jamas?' My husband is tactful when renewal requests from the Trademark Association arrive enquiring if we wish to preserve our tradename in Brazil. But at last I have an answer: real llamas, with soft fur, banana-shaped ears and Audrey Hepburn eyes.

Named Djuna Maria and Julio Jesus (pronounce that

Hoolio Haysoos please) I sing their names to them in my pretend Spanish in order to hark back to their Peruvian past, although they are from Wales and do not understand 'Buenos dias'. They prefer *Amazing Grace*, perhaps because I bought them from a Welsh American called Peter Bourne, a gentle doctor who persuaded Jimmy Carter to run for president, served on his staff and, a few years ago, bought a sheep farm in Wales where he keeps llamas.

When my llamas arrived there was no sign of Carter's sweet goodness. Although they never spit, they leapt like deer and avoided my gaze. But they enchanted me with their camel heads, split noses, harelips and two-toed feet.

And now they have succumbed to life at Wyken. We take them on evening walks to the vineyard and Djuna tickles my face with kisses that smell like fresh goats' cheese. Julio is still timid but Djuna is as leisurely and charming as a Southern belle.

If this was the Eighties I'd be marketing llama doo for compost and providing Nicole Farhi with llama fleeces for her winter collection. But it's the Nineties and I'm happy to sit in the old fruit cage, Rufus the cockerel on my lap, Djuna and Julio humming their plaintive hum and sniffing my ears. My sister says that the place 'looks like the Tijuana Zoo', and warns that I'll never get anywhere if I don't have ambition. I try to think of an answer but all that comes out is a sheepish hum.

June 18, 1998

A GENIUS OF THE LANGUAGE

IN her essay *The Quality of Travel*, Sybille Bedford writes: 'A part, a large part of travelling is an engagement of the ego v the world.' The world, 'hydra-headed and as old as the rocks', includes transport, the roads, messy money, keys, the waiters, the tourist industry, the weather. 'The ego,' she continues, 'wants to arrive at places safely and on time. It wants to be soothed, reassured, attended to, left in peace... It wants to be made to feel competent, generous, knowledgeable and of accepted looks. It wants to find everything just as it expected, only rather better.'

These words replay in my mind each time I arrange our quarterly dinners together. I'm now so stuck in the country that the world of London restaurants seems to me hydra-headed and rocky. We used to try different restaurants – La Fontana during the white truffle season, Turner's, The Ivy – but we have settled on Bibendum because it is not far from Sybille's flat in Chelsea, there are no stairs to antagonise her weak knee, everything is as expected and, once in a while, rather better.

Our friendship began in a literary way. I was writing about the *New Yorker's* Paris correspondent Janet Flanner, and Martha Gelborne suggested I meet Sybille. I had read most of Sybille's books, including her biography of Aldous Huxley, her books on law and justice, and her novels. I owned a copy of *A Legacy* with a quote from Nancy Mitford on its blue cover: 'I think it is one of the very best novels I have ever read'. My feelings exactly, so I jumped at the chance to meet the writer of what I believe is a masterpiece of 20th-century literature.

But ours has not been a literary friendship. What brought us together was a mutual passion for food and wine. Our memory bank includes scallops fresh from the Cornish sea, served with caramelised *endives*; plump pheasant moistened with leek sauce; meaty terrines of rabbit and hazelnut. One winter we drank our Tuesdays away at Steven Spurrier's Masterclasses in Wine at Christie's in South Kensington. Even now it's Sybille's verdict on my own wines that I value above anyone's.

When I say that Sybille is a genius of the English language, it is not an extravagance born of affection. After all, she has an OBE and is a fellow of the Royal Society of Literature. What is astonishing is that she is not English. Born in Charlottenburg, Germany, in 1911, she spent her early childhood in Baden and her adolescence in France and Italy. More than anyone I know she is a European.

Ten years ago we made a journey to Berlin. It was my first visit and her first return to the city for almost 50 years. She hated it. She disliked the cold, steely opulence of the modern streets, the nostalgic claustrophobia of the plush restaurants. So visible was her terror at Checkpoint Charlie as we negotiated a day-trip to East Germany, that I feared we would be held on suspicion. She did not relax until one evening we were taken to the Café de Paris, a French restaurant popular with German artists and film makers. This became her refuge and until we returned to London we ate every meal there (*entrecôte* properly grilled; *pommes frites*, slender and crisp and without grease; *Fleurie* served *frais.*)

But tonight's dinner at Bibendum is a celebration and we are joined by Alliette, who's come from Paris. Sybille has just recorded *Desert Island Discs* and over glasses of the house champagne we ask a flurry of questions: how long did the recording take? (two hours); what is Sue Lawley like? (knowledgeable and kind). While we try to guess Sybille's music, she reveals that Penguin is planning to reissue her novels, that she has begun work on a new book. I order more champagne. Sometimes life is rather better than expected.

June 25, 1998

BENTWATERS

'The centre of the village remains self-contained and quiet in spite of farm machines, motor-bikes and the dull murmur of summer holiday traffic on the bit of straight. Jets from the American base at Bentwaters occasionally ordain an immense sound and the place seems riven, splintered, yet it resumes its wholeness the second the plane vanishes. Nobody looks up.'

RONALD BLYTHE'S description of the American jets comes in his introduction to *Akenfield*, a portrait of a Suffolk coastal village as it was during the summer and autumn of 1967. Reading it 30 years on, what hits you is its timelessness.

Not that there haven't been changes in this bulge of East Anglia. For one thing, the jets stopped flying from Bentwaters five years ago, when American taxpayers began hankering after proof that the Cold War really was over. The Yanks had been here half a century, and most of that time they'd been courteous, considerate, even cultivated.

300

Early on they co-ordinated their flying schedule so that concerts, rehearsals and recordings at Snape Maltings would be undisturbed. Even during the Gulf War, flights of F111s were arranged so as not to drown out the haunting sea melodies of Benjamin Britten. The Americans were also appreciated for creating jobs on the base and for their relaxed spending habits locally. Happily, the closure of the base coincided with an upturn in tourists yearning for the bleak character of the landscape, the estuaries, the famous bird reserves and the long, shingly shores.

Meanwhile, the 1,000-acre site stood ominously empty and sealed off while rumours rumbled like the ghosts of jet engines. Transcendental Meditation's proposal for a university was turned down, plans for a Japanese factory never materialised. Then, in May 1997, it was announced that a Fred Mouawad had bought the site for a 'low key aviation facility'. In his press release he said he would 'fill the void' left by the Americans and bring Suffolk into the new millennium by creating a 'mutually supporting' International Airpark and Enterprise Park.

What he didn't say was that the new Bentwaters, located in one of two areas of Suffolk designated as Areas of Outstanding Natural Beauty, will be bigger than Birmingham Airport. That aircraft will take off or land at the airport every five minutes for 18 hours a day. Although he employed the justification proffered for every destructive or crass development on Earth –

employment – he did not say that the specialist workforce won't be the descendants of Akenfield.

Nor did he dwell on the price for his Skypark for 'businessmen flying to and from Europe and the holiday, charter season': a night sky obliterated by landing lights; crowded rural roads never meant for heavy traffic; noise, the relentless roar of engines. And, of course, silence: a world of music that will not survive the roar.

Walking along the ancient right of way from Aldeburgh to Snape, I recall that this is where I first heard Peter Pears, where I first saw *Peter Grimes*. Thoughts are sharpened in the ocean air. I chew over two: first, the prosaic, honourable words from the Government Planning Policy Guide: 'Sustainable development: not sacrificing what future generations will value for the sake of short-term and often illusory gains.'

And from the late Julian Tennyson, writing of the nearby village of Iken: 'Everyone wants to lie in his own country: this is mine. I shall feel safe if I have the scream of the birds and the moan of the wind and the lapping of the water all round me and the lonely woods and marshes I love so well.' He lies, not in Iken, but in the Burma jungle, where he was killed during the war against Japan. I do not believe we honour him if we take his dream away from future generations. Riven, splintered, this time the wholeness will not return.

July 9, 1998

302

THE HEALTH VISITOR

WHEN my friend Katie is too tired for words, she comes here to stay. That's how she describes her writer's block: too tired for words, a condition which is a handicap for a writer. She's just arrived with a broody hen she couldn't leave behind in Wales, her black labrador, Winston, and one of those battery-free radios that you crank up.

Katie is a bountiful guest. In the past she has come bearing 12 jars of her famous wild blackberry jam, a whole *jambon persillé*, a basket of four dozen candles made by her local candlemaker in North Wales. She brings good things for Sam, too: stilts she has made, invisible ink, a brass compass and books she finds at village fêtes. Last year she presented him with a scalpel and *Practical Taxidermy for Boys,* which begins: 'Let us suppose an owl has been lowering around suspiciously near the chicken coop, and that you have shot the rascal. Do not throw him away. What a splendid ornament he will make for the library!'

Today she has brought a wooden apple crate filled with bottles and bags. 'This will save your life,' she announces in her missionary voice as she arranges a display on the kitchen table: bottles of distilled white vinegar, washing soda, hydrogen peroxide, sodium perborate and 20 Mule Team Borax, two spray bottles and a small funnel. Somehow the arrangement lacks the glamour of beeswax candles and *jambon persillé*.

'Treat jostles with treat,' I say, trying to share her pride at the tablescape of products that look as though they belong in an early Edna O'Brien short story. She smiles with a sneaky look of wisdom and opens the cupboard beneath the kitchen sink. Out come the disinfectants. 'Cause brain damage, chest pains and cancer,' she chants, as the offending bottles go into the bin. 'All you need is borax and water. Light and air.' Then the window cleaner goes. 'Poison. Irritant to eyes and lungs. Use half water, half white wine vinegar in the pump spray.' Out goes my furniture polish, the kind used in stately homes. 'Damages liver, brain and kidney. Vegetable oil with Vitamin E as a preservative is just as effective.' Out goes my silver polish, the reward of a lengthy wait at Peter Jones. 'Remember,' snaps Katie, 'baking soda and water for silver; salt, flour and vinegar for brass; lemon juice and salt for copper.' Out goes the oven cleaner, drain cleaner and floor-polish. 'Mothballs are toxic to brain, liver and blood. Use cedar blocks and bags of lavender instead.'

I protest that I never use mothballs. 'Just warning you,' she replies.

I offer Katie a cup of coffee. To be on the safe side I make decaf. 'Hexane, which causes nerve damage, and methylene chloride, which causes cancer, are the chemicals used to decaffeinate coffee,' she explains under her breath.

In Katie's latest crime novel, housewives in the Midlands are dying at an epidemic rate. I don't want to give the plot away, but a serial killer, furniture polish, oven cleaner, farmed fish and tap water are all involved. The killer is never caught because the murder weapons are all self-inflicted household products. For three months Katie has worked with a team of environmental toxicologists so that everything is feasible and technically accurate.

'Look,' I tell my friend, 'just tell me the three worst things in my house.' Without hesitating she says: 'your mobile telephone, anything with artificial sweetener and fitted carpet. Oh, and don't stand in front of the microwave oven when it's on, towel dry your hair and go back to the manual typewriter.'

Suddenly the house seems booby-trapped, danger lurking everywhere. Katie assures me that really clean houses are the most dangerous and my mess is environmentally correct. I look at my bin filled with a museum of cleaning products. I feel too tired for words.

July 16, 1998

CONFESSIONS

MUCH has been made of the importance of travelling light. If you can pack for a two-week holiday in one of those little bags with wheels that qualify as 'carry on', then you will know an ecstasy of the kind granted only to Exclusive Brethren. I wouldn't know. I do not travel light. Not for me the religion of co-ordinates and wrinkle-free. I pack the day I leave and I have never been anywhere with fewer than three black skirts.

But it's not skirts that make my case too heavy to heave into overhead compartments. It's books. When I go to Ireland I take volumes of William Trevor, Seamus Heaney and Molly Keane. On trips to France I'm loaded down with old Pagnols, Colette, Mavis Gallant and Janet Flanner. Travel is confusing enough without reading William Faulkner in Italy or Virginia Woolf in Paris. That's why, when my cousin Jamelia sent me *Confessions of a Failed Southern Lady* at Christmas, I saved it for our summer holiday: an air-conditioned pilgrimage in a rented Buick across South Carolina, Georgia, Tennessee and Mississippi, staying with family and friends.

Our starting point is an island off the South Carolina coast to stay with my friend Rose. She comes down from Charlottesville for two weeks each summer. Still known as one of 'the Burks girls', Rose is what my grandmother called 'a born lady'. Signs of her innate ladyhood include her immaculate manners ('Manners', she tells her 17-year-old son, 'are thinking about others before you think about yourself'); her generous hospitality – Rose's table is revered in two countries; and dazzling elegance, whether she is wearing a faded T-shirt and size four shorts or vintage Chanel.

Rose's reading is rather highbrow and she claims she has never heard of *Confessions of a Failed Southern Lady*, or its author, fellow Virginian Florence King. Looking at its lipstick-pink cover, she whispers 'real ladies never confess'.

From my position in the hand-strung hammock for which Pawleys Island is famous, I cannot disagree. But Rose's remark sends me into a reverie about all the things my own grandmother tried to instil in me. Like Florence King's grandmother, she had given up on her own daughter, my mother, but she'd agree with Rose that confession isn't a lady thing. Not only is it unnecessary, it is 'introspective', the restless attendant of 'intellectual'.

In her career as ladysmith, my grandmother employed

the repetition method and I can still hear her now. Concerning dress, the most important thing was never to be overdressed: 'Just before you go out the door, take one thing off.' Walking into a room full of people: 'Always say the word blue as you enter, it makes you smile.' On conversation: 'Listen more than you talk. Nothing is so appealing as an intelligent silence.' It was her bad luck that I liked reading better than playing bridge, ran better than I strolled, preferred civil rights workers from the North to fraternity boys from Ole Miss, went to New England to college, took off for California, then to Paris, and never chose a silver pattern.

But just when my grandmother was convinced she would go to her grave having failed in her grand mission, a miracle occurred, a single event which wiped away a lifetime of crimes and misdemeanours. I was transformed from bohemian subversive to 'born lady': I married an Englishman. The change in my status was not my sole motive in marrying but, like a tax increase, it had immediate effect.

Lulled by the ocean breeze, I cannot say if my grandmother succeeded in making me a lady, but I'll say this in my defence: although I've talked more than I've listened, I've never entered a room without saying 'blue'. Or, as Florence King puts it: 'No matter which sex I went to bed with, I never smoked on the street'.

August 6, 1998

308

GRACELAND

WHEN harvest began here at Wyken this summer, I was at Graceland. As Robert Claydon's red Massey Ferguson combine began its stately glide through fields of Halcyon (yields 2.5 tons/acre, with 1.4% – 1.5% nitrogen; outside temperature 70°F), my husband, son and I were on the Platinum Tour (tickets $18.50 each, average time three hours, outside temperature 96°F).

This is what happens when you contract your farm. Someone else's combine pulls out of the farmyard at the crack of dawn while you climb aboard the *Lisa Marie* to see the bed where Elvis slept on flights to Las Vegas. You don't hear the thunderstorm that stops the harvest: you're listening to a neutral Acoustiguide voice reveal the promise Elvis made to his parents as a poor kid in Tupelo, Mississippi: 'One day, I'll make money, I'll be somebody and I'll take care of you. You won't have to work so hard – people will work for you. I'll buy you the prettiest house in Memphis.' Graceland, we are told, built in the

Georgian colonial style with Corinthian columns on the portico, is 'one American's dream fulfilled'.

Three hours due south of Graceland begins the Mississippi Delta. We are sitting on the long porch of my friend Celia's house, on top of the last hill before you reach the Delta, looking down on cotton fields still in the white blossom stage. When these hollyhock-like blooms drop off, the cotton bolls start to develop.

The Delta is the poorest part of Mississippi, which is the poorest state in the Union. The poverty has always been blamed on the agricultural identity of the state. Earlier in the day, an old friend, Billy Whittington, took us up in his twin-engined Cessna to see the Delta's newest crop: catfish. Acres and acres of catfish farms, spread out on the flat Delta plain where cotton is no longer king. Billy takes us up the Mississippi River. We fly so low we ought to be able to see catfish jumpin', so low we see our shadow on the levees that tame a river so wild that in 1927 it flooded an area the size of Scotland. Now miles of shallow fish farms make the Delta look like it's still under water.

Billy hasn't been lured by catfish. On his 2,600 acres, he's stayed with soybeans and cotton, both making good prices now. Although his house in the middle of a cotton field is bigger than Graceland, Billy lives cautiously. He remembers rockbottom cotton prices in the Eighties when the Chinese started producing cotton, advised by Delta planters. He now sees plummeting grain prices fuelled by foreign competition, farmers who still haven't recovered from the years of floods and soggy fields that have saddled wheat and barley crops with disease. Signs on the grain elevators across the prairies read: *Times are so tough that even the people who don't intend to pay aren't buying.*

Once there was a lull between events in America and their arrival in Britain. Global markets have abbreviated that pause and the free-falling prices for wheat, barley, peas, beans, cattle and pigs are echoed here. Throughout the UK, pig farmers are losing £30 per pig as supermarkets sell imported pork at giveaway prices. It doesn't matter if you're in Suffolk or Kansas, the message is the same: there's no way to keep producing milk, wheat, pigs or cattle at today's prices and survive.

Farmers are always painting apocalyptic visions, complains Celia's son, Wyatt. He grows newspapers, not cotton. As we watch a blazing sun set over the Delta, we talk Graceland and the American dream, culture and agriculture. Wyatt strums an old guitar and Elvis gives way to Don McLean as we begin to sing the one song we all know: *Drove my Chevy to the levee but the levee was dry... them good ol' boys were drinking whiskey and rye, singing 'This'll be the day that I die...'*

August 13, 1998

DELIVERANCE

DAWN is rather like a dinner party. I always hate the idea of it, but when I get there I generally have a pretty good time. This morning I see a whole new side of country life in the nearby village of Ixworth: the familiar start-and-stop serenade of the milk float; the procession of scruffy cats strolling homeward down the empty street; a lone, sparky boy on rollerblades delivering fresh copies of *The Daily Telegraph*.

I'm waiting in front of The Pickerel for the private bus service that takes country dwellers to London each morning: £12.50 a round trip, stops at Liverpool Street, Whitehall, Victoria and anywhere else you request *en route*. Half the price of the train and less effort, the bus is like a club where everyone knows each other.

I'm going up to London because it's moving day. Sam's godmother, Valerie, has sold her flat on the King's Road in World's End (four-room maisonette, roof terrace and sit-in kitchen) and is moving to a three-room flat with galley kitchen and balcony in Elm Park Gardens. Now she will have a large, peaceful room that looks out onto trees. Plus all the stuff that filled up her old flat.

My role today is provider of moral support. She already has an impressive team of moving men to load boxes and cart furniture. I arrive with *café lattes* and banana muffins from the Seattle Coffee Company and tell her that she is doing the right thing.

I help in the editing process, filling up black bin bags and taking them to the Oxfam shop round the corner, fishing out a few of the edited items on the way: a Chanel T-shirt bought on the beach in Mauritius; bottles of scent still in their boxes from an old boyfriend who believed in duty-free shops; those plain white notebooks you start and never continue. The little clock with blue enamelled numerals that's never worked is now mine. I stop only because I know I will never get all this stuff back to the bus in the evening. Actually, I stop because I'm supposed to be comforting my friend.

'This is a shipwreck,' she moans. 'I've been getting rid of stuff all week and it looks like I've done nothing.' We walk from room to room, staring at piles of belongings, the flotsam and jetsam of daily life. I chose Valerie as godmother to my child because she is one of my oldest and closest friends, but also because she operates on a more spiritual level than I do. I am acquisitive, she is inquisitive; she understands quantum physics and the importance of dreams. She calls me the Duchess of Terra Firma. If I had a coat of arms my motto would read 'Having is Believing'.

Still we shuffle piles round. Coats, books, woks, lamps, shoes, pictures, are banished to the Oxfam pile, given a reprieve, condemned again. A cloud of despair hangs over us. I continue to chant 'you've done the right thing', as I nervously survey the rooms she has sacrificed for one room with a view. I think of my own mountain of possessions, rising ever higher as I have country space. Everyone I know complains of drowning in a sea of possessions.

I think of the old Yiddish saying: 'Three moves is like a fire', and would add, 'but no moves is like quicksand'. A few years back I condemned Jackie Kennedy's children when they sold all their mother's stuff at Sotheby's. Let me rephrase that: I understand the ordinary peace of cupboards cleared, the seduction of empty rooms.

As I speculate on the meaning of our desire to acquire, Valerie persuades the movers to delay delivery. The vans will spend the weekend in the warehouse so that she can spend the first four days in her new flat in empty rooms. 'All the better to edit out the extraneous,' she says. We stop to buy champagne to toast her new home. Sitting on the floor it feels wonderfully clutter-free and urban. We rely on the poet Anne Stevenson for our first toast: *As the furniture heaves off your life, you'll love your deliverance.*

August 20, 1998

SORREEE

SOME things make me stop whatever I'm doing and just listen. *Thought for the Day* does it when Bishop Harries or Charles Handy make a rare reappearance. *Death and the Maiden* by Schubert. *The Battle Hymn of the Republic. Letter from America.* It was during one of those moments of pure concentration that I learned something valuable from Alistair Cooke. He was quoting Mark Twain who said that 'the difference between the right word and the nearly right word is the difference between lightning and lightning bugs'.

That little nugget of truth lodged itself in my mind. A lot of the time I feel like making do with the nearly right word so that I can get on and do something else, but then my ear gets struck by a flicker of internal lightning. Which is not the same as getting struck by lightning bugs.

Mark Twain came back to me this morning at 3:08am after President Clinton had addressed the American people and anyone else who could stay up and watch

BBC1 All-night News. It was that word 'appropriate'. He said that he'd had 'a relationship that wasn't appropriate'. Maybe three in the morning's not my hour, maybe I missed something, but 'appropriate' – as in 'inappropriate' – just didn't sound appropriate to me. I'm not saying that a tearful confession was required but something along the lines of 'I was wrong and I am sorry' would have felt better to my ears.

The problem is, 'I am sorry' has somehow fallen into the category of antiquated usage. It's not current, not cool, not accepted use. The word has slipped from its first dictionary definition – an adjective 'expressing or feeling pity, sympathy, remorse, grief or regret' – to its third meaning, 'poor or paltry', as in 'a sorry excuse'. And now there is an entire generation unaware of its adjectival role, who knows it only as an exclamation of apology that hovers between aggressive and meaningless: 'Sorry'.

Sorry, but I think 'Sorry' stinks. It may be acceptable when you realise you've been hogging the aisle at Waitrose and your fellow shoppers cannot pass, but it is not adequate when you back into the car behind you in the car park. Variations get even worse: 'Sorry about that' and 'Sorreee' mean the opposite: I am not in the least sorry. Sorry.

The origins of vanishing remorse – in thought, word and deed – are unclear. Social historians blame the rise of litigation: to apologise is to admit guilt, which means you will be held responsible and you will pay. I trace the collapse to a more prosaic source, to the opening line of *Love Story*: 'Love means never having to say you're sorry.' The movie appeared when this present generation of politicians were at university, and whereas concepts of Keynesian Economics and Domino Theory remained impenetrable, this one stuck.

Lord Carrington, pre-*Love Story*, will go down in history as the last English politician to say – and mean – he was sorry. He also understood that genuine remorse requires an act as sincere as resignation, not a word-shuffle to buy more time to brazen it out.

When my nine-year-old breaks a window with his catapult, I expect him to say 'I'm sorry, Mama.' I can't make him feel remorse but if he doesn't know the language of regret, he'll never know how it feels. The root of his sorrow may be the knowledge that the weapon will be confiscated. That's tough but it's all part of learning about conduct, fundamental decencies, the difference between stupid and wrong. At least he isn't going to tell me that he used his catapult in an inappropriate way. And he's not going to use the exclamation 'Sorry!' Even Sam knows that the difference between 'I am sorry' and 'Sorry' is the difference between lightning and lightning bugs.

August 27, 1998

NATURE V NURTURE

THIS is not the martyr I meant to be. My idea of martyrdom has always hovered between Jeanne d'Arc, the Jean Seberg version, and Rosa Luxemburg. Never did my dreams extend to the torture of a rainy afternoon at Rollerbury with the thunder of skaters whizzing by to the music of Prodigy.

We're in a barrack in a rundown part of town, wedged in between the Club Brasilia and the Bury St Edmunds train station, a class-free time warp that smells of feet, Coca-Cola and Lysol. It's the classlessness that stands out. In the blur of tattooed fathers, tired mothers and pale children, I recognise Freddie, son of the Prince of Wales's architect, and a beautiful young girl named Portia wearing a 'Vassar' T-shirt, her opera-singer mother's Alma Mater. But most of the messages proclaim the Zero Class society: Tommy Hilfiger sweatshirts and Liverpool football strips. My son and his friend Chris are dressed in identical khakis and navy blue GAP sweatshirts.

The martyrs I most admire are the mothers clutching the small hands of their solemn toddlers as they guide them round the rink. These mothers are earning Good Mom cards. I'm the Bad Mom, only tempted to put on rollerblades for the three minutes it takes Whitney Houston to sing *I Will Always Love You* from *The Bodyguard*. Instead, I return to my vending-machine cappuccino and pull out my copy of *The New Yorker*. I've been trying all week to finish the cover story: 'Why Parents Don't Matter', a 'startling new theory about what really makes kids turn out the way they do'.

The article is based on a book written by psychologist and grandmother Judith Rich Harris. Kicked out of graduate school because she lacked 'originality and independence', Mrs Harris has produced what many serious thinkers claim is the most revolutionary thought of our time: that in the classic debate over Nature (genes) versus Nurture (devoted, competent parents who sit at Rollerbury rather than surrender to Nintendo), the Nurture equation is all wrong. Harris maintains that a child's behaviour is 50% genetic (more or less) and 50% peer group. Environmentalists like Freud and Philip Larkin got it wrong: it's not what 'your mum and dad' do that shapes the behaviour of children, but what friends and classmates do.

The book, called *The Nurture Assumption*, is due out this autumn, and its radical message is twofold: first, that a child's personality – what we used to call 'character' – is not shaped by the parents; and second, what's important is not what children learn inside the home but what they learn outside the home.

The implications of this thinking for our parent-obsessed culture are staggering. If embraced, it could wipe out maternal guilt felt by working and non-working mothers alike. Nanny-guilt would go, as well as my personal speciality: guilt at sending my son to boarding school, not nurturing him seven nights a week. And then there are wider conclusions: a child living in a troubled family in a good neighbourhood is better off than a child living in a good family in a troubled neighbourhood.

As the summer holidays wind down, this sounds like liberation theology: the blame – and the credit – should be spread out, onto schools, neighbourhoods, peers and the children themselves. I'm sorry for the novelists and psychotherapists who will be put out of work by this idea, but I like to think that you can have a child without surrendering your entire emotional existence for a 20-year chunk.

As I watch my son enter the long, straight stretch, I feel the urge to coach from the sideline: 'Lean forward, bend your knees'. But Sam avoids my gaze. Skating alongside his friend Chris, he seamlessly picks up the principles of gravity and balance. As Mrs Harris might observe: Chris is a skater of speed and grace.

September 3, 1998

MUTUAL DEPENDANCE

A COUPLE of years ago, during the halcyon days of school runs through potato fields to his pre-prep school, I heard Sam tell his back-seat colleague: 'My mother doesn't have a job'. This was a revelation to me and I was tempted to butt in and set him straight but I kept quiet as he explained: 'My papa works and my mother stays up late.'

That version of my employment status came back to me this week when I was asked if I would be on one of those chat show radio programmes. The subject: Working Mothers in the Countryside. Flattered as I was to be considered a Working Mother, I declined to partake. I have a thing about the epidemic of folks chatting on the radio, and as a Working Mother, the thought of driving to Northampton where BBC Midlands is produced is enough to render me speechless.

Still, the invitation got me thinking about what I would have said. First, I might have looked at working mothers from Sam's viewpoint. I don't wear a uniform (mothers who wear a nurse's uniform rate very highly) and I don't go to an office. I don't have a job title: dentist, doctor, lawyer, Jungian analyst. True, I run a vineyard, a country store and a vineyard restaurant and I work hard in all three places, but I also have staff. And, yes, I stay up late, as Sam said. Even now I'm writing this sitting in a quiet house where dogs, cats, children, husband sleep. I can see how, to objective eyes, I don't have a job.

It's hard to have a job in the country. So much time is spent in a car, so many people come to stay, so many creatures – furred, feathered, human – require feeding, that having a job (or two, three, four) that is unrecognised, unpaid and untitled is normal. Every country woman I know is either worn out from combining work with country and family life, or feels guilty because she doesn't have a job. And what they all want is the impossible: a job that takes place during school hours and magically halts during school holidays.

I've worked almost since Sam was born, and I've been rather smug about never having a nanny. If I'd gone on radio I think I'd have been pushed to tell the truth: I never had *au pairs* or nannies because, from the time Sam was a year old, I had Pat. Today, while I pulled suckers off vines, planned menus with the restaurant chef, studied budgets with the accountant and took the first sugar readings of the grapes, Pat drove Sam to Ben's birthday party, collected Alder Carr fruit ice-creams for the restaurant, did the food shopping for the weekend. Tomorrow she will finish sewing in any nametags I've missed, collect Sam's guitar from the music shop, feed and water the sheep.

Granddaughter of a vicar and a gamekeeper, and daughter of a tea-planter in Africa, Pat is patient, resourceful and, above all, flexible. If I'd agreed to go to Northampton she would have driven me there. But above all, Pat has been a stable fixture in Sam's life since he was a year old. She likes to polish tables but she isn't a cleaner; she makes a dazzling fruit salad but she's not the cook; she's a member of our household but she lives in a farm cottage with her husband and, from time to time, her grown children. She is our Creator of Order.

I know that I could not be whatever it is I am, if I didn't have Pat to do the things that give me peace of mind while I work and earn money. Pat is what every woman needs: a paid member of the family. Plus she is good-natured, tolerant, mechanical, solid. The only serious disagreement we ever had was after Diana appeared on *Panorama*. We were both astonished at each other's vehemence.

It is now just after midnight and Sam's mother is up late. It doesn't feel like a job but this is what I do. I'm a Working Mother in the Country, thanks to another Working Mother in the Country. It is a relationship of genuine mutual dependence, and it works.

September 10, 1998

FRENCH LEAVE

IN what I shall some day describe as my 'early English years', my horizons were principally those of the No 19 bus. When you regularly travel a bus route you begin to recognise faces. Every week or so I would encounter a tallish, passive man in a corduroy jacket and sad shoes who always muttered the same question: 'Why did I ever leave Paris? Why did I ever leave Paris?' I had only recently learned not to catch the eye of such haunted people, but this man's repetitive regret has stuck with me over the years as surely as if he had followed me home.

Sometimes this sad lament comes back to me out of the blue. Biting into an early Worcester Pearmain windfall in the middle of the apple orchard, I suddenly yearn for the taste and smell of hot chestnuts in the Tuileries. Gazing at the blood red dahlias that light up the red hot border, I can think only of the pleasure of spending ten *francs* on a bunch of indigo purple anemones to put in an old Dijon mustard pot. Drinking tea by the Aga and reading the *East*

Anglian Daily Times, I feel overcome with the desire to be leaning against the bar in my old café near Métro Alésia, reading *Le Monde* over an *express*.

What triggers my *nostalgie* for *temps perdu* is autumn, the time of year when Paris and Parisians are at their best: cheerful after their holidays, confident in their new clothes. In the English countryside there is not the same *esprit de rentrée* in the local market town, where you embark on the school shoe mission followed by its dubious reward: lunch at Pizza Hut.

I hadn't quite begun to mumble 'Why did I ever leave Paris? Why did I ever leave Paris?' as I studied the shoe section of the Boys' Clothing and Equipment List – one pair black outdoor shoes, one pair white gym shoes, one pair trainers, one pair football boots (rubber studs only), one pair wellington boots – but introspective yearnings stirred inside me. And then, like a traveller in the desert who stumbles upon an oasis, I saw mine: a zinc bar, newspapers on poles, a basket of croissants. Afraid that this was a cruel mirage, I pulled Sam in with me. What we saw was beautiful and real: the old Sun Alliance building, Grade II listed, meticulously converted into a French café, down to the walls and ceiling painted a reassuring nicotine cream.

Okay, not a *vrai* French café, but the Café Rouge, part of a chain that is spreading beyond its urban origins of London. I saw my reflection in the mirror behind the bar, in the beaming brass espresso machine.

Usually I despair of the progress that has rewarded Bury St Edmunds with Monsoon, Early Learning Centre, Body Shop, Superdrug, Hush Puppies, Jumpers, Dixons and 20 or so other shops destined to blot out any sense of uniqueness in this most charming English market town. But on this day I climbed off my high horse and sat down.

I ordered *pain au chocolat* and croissants, cappuccino and *chocolat chaud*. I did not expect to look up and see Simone de Beauvoir sitting upright and alone, as I once did in the Select. Nor was there the buzz and graceful movement of experienced waiters that accompanies a *grand crême* at the Coupole, but Sam was good company, the croissants tasted like the real thing and the coffee was rather better than memory.

In a few days I may complain again about the 'multiples' that insidiously devour a town's identity, depriving its citizens of a sense of place. I will steadfastly patronise the New Saxon Bookshop over W H Smith. But the truth is, what I've missed most about country life are places to sit, drink coffee, be anonymous, make lists, read the paper and, above all, feel that you are somewhere. As writer and country dweller Flannery O'Connor put it: 'Somewhere is better than anywhere.'

September 17, 1998

A FAREWELL TO FARMS

WE are sitting in the kitchen drinking Italian roast coffee
and giving away our sheep. Our Lincoln Longwools to be
precise: the large white sheep with Rastafarian dreadlocks
that cover their gentle eyes. The Lincolns look like Mary's
little lamb on steroids: white, curly, adorable and
gargantuan. Ours have won us prizes at the Suffolk Show,
made us laugh with their quizzical looks, knocked us over
in their passion for molasses pellets, kept us up through
the night with birthing problems and infuriated us with
their tendency to lie down and crush their lambs.

Which was no reason to banish them. The idea that
we should get rid of the sheep was my husband's. Over
the years he has listened patiently as our accountant,
Mr Durrant, described our sheep as 'on the brink of
commercial ascendancy', but now he has lost heart. I
am not wounded by words like 'ornamental' and
'uneconomic'. Mutterings about Marie Antoinette do not
injure my pride: I simply refuse to live on a farm without

a farm animal in view. So we compromised: we would downsize, the Lincolns would go but the wild and picturesque Jacobs and the intelligent and companiable Shetlands would be reprieved.

In fact, I suspected the fate of the Lincolns was sealed months ago when we decided to contract out the farm. Sheep are not an attraction in Suffolk prairieland and it was clear through interview after interview that no farmer interested in farming at Wyken had any interest in livestock. The day-to-day shepherding fell to me on March 1st, assisted by Heather, a fourth generation Suffolk shepherd who comes here once a week to help trim feet, check for disease, organise shearing and dipping.

I love sheep. I love looking out onto a field and seeing their biblical silhouettes munching the grass. I love going out to the barn in the middle of the night just to check, and hearing a little bleat. I feel maternal pride as I praise the ewe on her achievement, swab baby belly buttons with iodine before sitting beside the new mama and studying what nature and breeding and care and time have led to. I also love tweed suits, sheepskin slippers, pink leg of lamb with rosemary and garlic, and wool blankets but, at the moment of birth, I just feel honoured to be in the neighbourhood of a miracle of instinct and evolution.

I'm a lucky woman. I can afford a few ornamental sheep. Real sheep farmers can't. That's why farmers in Shetland are faced with the heartbreaking prospect of shooting up to 20,000 sheep. These are farmers with no market for their sheep, no winter feed and no signs of hope that the collapse in the market, the tyranny of supermarket power and insane and unscientific food scares will end. This is a terrible tragedy for farmers who believe they have no choice but to humanely slaughter their animals and bury them in pits.

It's not just the sheep that will go. The island and hill farmers will also disappear. Like miners whose sons stayed out of the pits, these farmers will not be followed by members of their family. The large-scale abandonment of land has begun.

Last week, we placed an ad for our flock of Lincolns in *The Ark*. Our only reply was from a 76-year-old farmer in Norwich, a former Japanese prisoner-of-war who wants a ram to breed with his Merinos to see if he can get more length into the fleece. After choosing a ram lamb and agreeing a price, we decided to just give him the ram.

And now we're giving the rest of the Lincolns to Heather who will breed them with her Suffolks. We will see them living out their woolly lives down the road at Stowlangtoft. We're no longer on the brink of commercial ascendancy but we don't have to kill and bury our sheep. Compared with the plight of hill farmers, giving away your sheep is a luxury of epic proportions.

October 1, 1998

WEEKENDERS

'THEY arrive in their midnight blue Saab on Friday night, unload their boxes of food from the King's Road branch of Waitrose, and never set foot in the pub or village shop. The only money they spend in the village is on the Sunday papers and the cleaner who comes on Fridays.' Isobel is in full rant as we pick grapes on a clear October day. The objects of her ire are the new owners of the Old Rectory. 'Londoners,' she spits as she dumps her full buckets into the black bins.

I don't point out to Isobel that she was educated at St Paul's, married at St Margaret's and gave birth at Queen Charlotte's. There's no point in debating the merits of Waitrose on the King's Road versus Waitrose in Bury St Edmunds for buying your hunks of Parmesan Reggiano. I pay my pickers by the hour, not the basket, and I'd rather discuss the thorny issue of weekenders when it's not my nickel.

Still, as I roam the rows checking the grapes in my role

as quality control officer, I rehearse my arguments. In the cluster of villages that surrounds the vineyard, I know dozens of full-time, dedicated country dwellers who began their Suffolk lives as weekenders. Some, like Jean and Francine, bought their cottage in Troston when their sons, Max and Jacques, were babies. When the boys reached school age they left London. My friend Jorn bought his cottage 30 years ago and spent his weekends here until he retired from Christian Dior. Now he lives at Hillwatering during the week and spends his weekends in London. This reversal of the notion of the country weekend is becoming a social trend. Other friends, Charles and Liz Handy, spend their weekdays in Norfolk and their weekends in Putney.

Charles is a philosopher who writes books that sell millions of copies. Most people think that writers can live anywhere, and even I try to persuade myself that the best place is an idea. Still, Charles's writing room in their cottage near Diss seems to me the perfect writer's room: a cathedral-like space where he produces his unique blend of shrewd, scholarly, thoughtful analysis about the world we live in. In his most recent book, *The Hungry Spirit*, he describes the view from his writing room, an idyllic pastoral scene of fields and woods that hasn't changed in 100 years. 'Some things don't change,' he writes. 'In the village behind me, people fall in love, breed children, walk their dogs and gossip about their neighbours, just as they've always done. The great themes of life with which we all have to deal – love and death, loneliness and responsibility – are still with us.' He then says that appearances can also lie. That a century ago two men scythed the crop on those fields at the rate of an acre a day. Now, one man does 20 acres a day, on contract.

People in the Handy's village don't work on the land any more: they work for Japanese banks and computer firms, for London publishers and estate agents. Cottages that once housed two families of farmworkers now are equipped with computers, modems, fax machines and burglar alarms and perhaps a single young woman like the one I met last night at dinner. Lauren works for a merchant bank in London from her cottage down a mile-long private track. When I asked her about her job she explained: 'I manage the national debt of Lebanon.'

Times are changing and, like it or not, the countryside has to change, too. We can lament the increasing suburbanisation of market towns and villages, and we have to fight to preserve what agricultural life we have left. But we cannot prolong the past. The truth is, Constable country is far more interesting today than it was when Constable was painting it. When weekend dwellers become – as more and more do – full-time country folk, they bring a creative, exhilarating spirit to rural life. They are also world-class grape-pickers.

October 22, 1998

MAN AND PIG

WHAT follows may be upsetting, so close your eyes if you are squeamish. The subject is pigs.

Pigs. If you have ever kept any of the five main farm animals – sheep, chickens, cows, horses, pigs – you will know that the pig is the most intelligent, and the most sensitive. Folks like to think that the horse is, and I admit that there is a majesty in horses that overwhelms the human heart. But pigs are smart, so smart that scientists trying to understand human behaviour turn to pigs.

Which might make you think that humans have a lot of respect for pigs. Treat them humanely. And once upon a time you'd have been right. In the 1950s, when the price of land was £100 an acre, farmers round here kept sows out in the fields. Sometimes you'd see as many as 100 sows surrounded by their piglets. Pigs weren't as demanding as cows: you needed only simple huts and fencing, and your main investment was a good boar. Any pig farmer will tell you that a good boar, like a bull, is 50% of your herd.

Those were happy days, when man and pig lived in sunshine and harmony. It's true the pig became bacon and the farmer did not, but the farmer was grateful and the pig was not unhappy. And then came Change. First there was the introduction of the import levies with the Common Agricultural Policy which caused the price of land to skyrocket. Then the Ministry of Agriculture introduced grants and subsidies to take out hedges, lay down concrete, put up buildings, accompanied by tax allowances for fittings and equipment.

Suddenly, outdoor pigs, known as 'extensive' farming, didn't make economic sense. What made sense were highly subsidised indoor pigs, known as 'intensive' systems. Within five years 90% of all sows were placed in indoor stalls, each in a kind of iron-bar cage only inches longer and wider than the sow herself. She was kept here from the time she was served by the boar until she was removed to the farrowing pen, a period of four months. During this time she never left her stall. She could stand up or lie down, but she couldn't move forward or turn round. In January 1999 this system, called 'stall and tethering', will be illegal in the UK. Already most producers have phased it out.

Which doesn't mean that a sow's life is great. Come farrowing time she's removed to a pen and held in a metal-barred crate where she cannot turn round. Her maternal instinct – to build a nest for her piglets – is frustrated, and she is kept in this prison until the piglets are taken away at three to four weeks.

It sounds appalling but the truth is that nowhere in the world are pigs farmed with higher standards of welfare than in Britain. Huge progress has been made here (thanks to intrepid campaigners such as Sir Richard Body) and the welfare of pigs is improving every year. The problem is, there may not be any British pigs if things continue the way they are going. Every week dozens of pig farmers are forced by the banks to slaughter their loss-making pigs. In some parts of Suffolk even pregnant sows are now being slaughtered as pig farmers go under.

History shows that when a nation's agriculture goes wrong, the rest of the nation's life goes wrong too. Agriculture weaves through our lives like a vast river, its tributaries affecting our health, our landscape, our wildlife, all the material things that matter to us. And it's now going wrong. Supermarkets are choosing cheap, imported bacon, ham and sausages over British pork. The EU forbids labels which tell the consumer where the meat is from. We must prepare for a healthy little trade war. We can begin by boycotting supermarkets and restaurants that sell any pork other than British. If British pig farmers disappear, the blow to the nation's life will be great. The blow to compassionate farming and animal welfare will be incalculable.

October 1, 1998

THE COOL INVENTORY

THE hero in Nick Hornby's newest novel *About a Boy* fills out a magazine questionnaire in search of the 'cool' profile of its readers. How cool was Will Leitmann? This cool: in the last three months he had slept with a woman he didn't know very well (five points). He had spent more than £300 on a jacket (five points). He had spent more than £20 on a haircut (five points). He had eaten in a restaurant that serves polenta and shaved Parmesan (five points). By the time Will completes the questionnaire it is clear that he is so cool he could die from hypothermia.

Actually, I haven't read the book (deduct two points) but I read the big hunk of it published in the Christmas issue of *The New Yorker* (three points) and I've been doing my own 'cool' inventory ever since. For instance: I wear a lot of grey (five points) but no Nicole Farhi (deduct five). I own a restaurant that serves polenta and shaved Parmesan (ten points), but my customers prefer potatoes to polenta (deduct five). I live on a farm but I don't drive a four-wheel drive vehicle (five points); I drive a Volvo (deduct five). I've never voted Conservative in my life (ten points); I married a Conservative MP (deduct ten).

All the same, I've always felt that I was cool. At least coolish. Cool compared to my adorable but not very cool husband. Cool... until today. As we were finding our seats for the half-term concert at Sam's prep school, the headmaster greeted us and asked if he could have a quiet word afterwards. A long hour later, *Michael Row the Boat Ashore* still singing in my head, Mr Auster told us that Sam had had a good beginning term, done some lovely work, but that 'Matron overheard Sam use the f-word, and if you could just reinforce the no-swearing rule...'

Suddenly I felt the queen of uncool. I did not think 'Well, what do you expect when Richard Branson (old cool) uses the f-word on the *Today* programme and, asked by an astonished journalist if he would like to rephrase his comment, repeats it?' Nor did I feel like pointing out that my brand new *Oxford Dictionary* has ten entries for the f-word, spelled out without stars, euphemisms or asterisks, but right there in print as plain as a poem by Philip Larkin memorised for A-level English.

My earliest palate memory is the taste of Ivory soap, used persistently by my parents in an effort to wash the word 'damn' from my mouth where it got firmly lodged, aged two. By the time I entered motherhood, the Ivory soap method was considered child abuse. When I heard my toddler mutter 'Oh God' when he spilled his Smarties or struggled with Duplo, I realised the only effective method was to erase the phrase from my own vocabulary.

Dealing with the f-word is trickier and what I understand now is that parenthood makes me an honorary member of the counter-culture. My job is to counter the culture that holds that the f-word is the verb of cool. Despite its proliferation in the cool world of football and film I have to convince Sam that the f-word is totally uncool, the Ribena of the language. It may not be on the list of taboos that you never, never do like Lie, Steal, Bully, and it may feel cool to say forbidden words (and I know the feeling), but you just don't do it.

As headmasters go, Sam's is pretty cool. He has a son at Shrewsbury which probably helps. Meanwhile, Sam is adamant that he doesn't believe that 'rude words are cool'. I know he wants to be cool and I hope I can convince him that playing B. B. King on his guitar, being the A-team goalie, even writing his essays on a laptop are all 'well cool'. He wears his Kangol cap backwards (five points) and can do 'Rock the baby on the trapeze' with his yoyo (five points). And, in case you are wondering, Sam can't be bothered to read the back page of COUNTRY LIFE (five points).

November 5, 1998

THE REMARKABLE MR. CARRIER

STUCK on my refrigerator door is an advertisement that I clipped out of *The Daily Telegraph* last week. It's the Quote of the Day from Corby Trouser Press: 'As I hurtled through space, one thought kept crossing my mind – every part of this capsule was supplied by the lowest bidder.' John Glenn. The quote appeared the day Glenn was launched on his return trip into space nearly 30 years later, at the age of 77.

The better-known moon quote, made by Neil Armstrong when he climbed out of the Apollo spacecraft and bounced on the moon – 'That's one small step for man, one giant leap for mankind' – never made it to the fridge doors of my mind. There is something about return trips and the redefining of 'the prime of life' that I find more compelling.

Which is why I spent two days this week searching linen chests and airing cupboards for our mountain of damask tablecloths, not used since Christmas. Mainly I'm content to eat on the polished oak table, but this was a grand occasion: a dinner celebrating the birthday of our tenant who lives in the cottage that overlooks our vineyard. He is the John Glenn of our East Anglian universe: a shockingly youthful 75-year-old, whose face and *esprit de corps* have defied gravity with lunar-like perfection, and whose return trip to Suffolk four years ago, after a decade away, has been just as remarkable.

Most people know Robert Carrier for his *Great Dishes of the World*, in its day the best-selling cookbook of all time. Carrier was an altogether more worldly and glamourous Delia, and his handsome looks, lion's share of vitality and passion for good food transformed England's culinary horizon. Fiercely intelligent – he was a cryptographer with American Intelligence during the Second World War – he brought an American sense of glamour and fun to English food writing. Like the other great food writers of the 1970s and 80s – Elizabeth David, whom he succeeded as food editor of *Harpers' Bazaar*, and Jane Grigson – Robert Carrier's first culinary conversion took place in France. But as a survivor of the Battle of the Bulge, his knowledge of the Gallic *terroir* was never purely intellectual. Nor was he ever a tourist in France. After the war he went to Paris to edit a Gaullist magazine and when it folded he retreated to his *maison secondaire* in St Tropez, where he learned to cook from an intrepid French restaurateur. The legendary Fifine disguised her Carrier rehabilitation programme as omelette lessons.

340

I first ate at Carrier's in Islington in the early 1980s. I began with the famous cucumber salad (better than caviar) and ended with Mrs Moxon's lemon posset. I knew his famous country-house restaurant Hintlesham Hall only from the photographs in *Terence Conran's Kitchen Book*. When I moved to Suffolk, it had been sold and there were rumours that Carrier was living in Morocco, New York, Paris (all true).

And then, at the age of 70, Robert came back to England, rented a flat in London, and renewed contacts in his old worlds of food, publishing and television. But he was still hankering after Suffolk. He moved into our cottage, put in a new kitchen and entered a period of phenomenal creativity. In four years he has written and published five books, including his *New Great Dishes of the World* which he photographed. He has filmed four television series in his cottage kitchen.

Robert also dispenses free advice when I have restaurant problems, sits in on interviews with chefs, tests recipes and stoically accepts that his drive is a mud hole during the sugar beet season. Like John Glenn, he still navigates the world, but his quest is for great dishes. And for the curious reader: the damask tablecloths were found, moon-coloured with age, a perfect canvas for a menu of oyster bisque, poached rabbit and Mrs Moxon's lemon posset. Many happy returns, dear Robert.

November 26, 1998

341

HOLIDAY INN

MY Great-Aunt Edna (aged 93) is worried about my Great-Aunt Blanche (95). On the telephone she says quietly: 'I think Blanche has Alzheimer's.'

'Oh no,' I murmur. 'She was so sharp when we spent the day with her at the old people's home this summer.'

'She says she can't tell one Christmas from another; they all run together in a blur. And now she wants to spend Christmas in a hotel.'

I feel honour-bound to comfort my Aunt Edna, despite my own blur of Christmases past. I also understand the hotel thing. I have guilty Christmas hotel fantasies myself: country inns perched on mountains in Vermont or Switzerland, or temples to immaculate service, like Cliveden. I don't dream of a White Christmas, I dream of Christmas with white linen sheets, changed invisibly while I'm having breakfast or sitting with the papers beside a warming fire whose success has nothing to do with my effort. This dream includes midnight mass at a nearby cathedral, with carols sung in a foreign language, a mist of incense, devout believers wearing fur hats. On reflection, I gently suggest to my Aunt Edna that maybe Aunt Blanche isn't losing her mind but searching for a higher truth.

Still, it's curious. To my knowledge, Aunt Blanche has never stayed in a hotel in her life. According to Aunt Edna, her sister has decided that this is going to be her last Christmas and she doesn't want to spend it in a place that is all on one level, sitting on plastic-covered chairs, surrounded by wilting poinsettias and people older than she is, most of whom are Baptists.

Aunt Blanche has a thing about Baptists. She's a Methodist who taught me the difference between the Protestant denominations. A Methodist is a Baptist who has learned to read; a Presbyterian is a Methodist who has moved to town; and an Episcopalian is a Presbyterian who has got rich. Blanche brought the same clarity to her theories of redemption. Once saved through immersion, the Baptists were always saved; Methodists could fall from grace; and Presbyterians were born into salvation. Blanche was devout, but not humourless. One summer, my cousins and I acquired a glow-in-the-dark sign at Methodist church camp which we nailed to the gate that led from Edna's garden into Blanche's: 'Wide is the gate, narrow the path and very few shall enter therein.' It stayed in place until Hurricane Hugo blew the fence away.

Aunt Blanche's house is still there, a modest museum to her past life, dusted and polished once a week by Lucidity (aged 82). Next door to Edna's, and across the road from my grandmother's, the trio of houses lived in by the three sisters is a landmark, built for them by my grandfather in 1920. Surely, I suggest, her grandchildren and great-grandchildren could be prevailed upon to open up her house, disguise the smell of mildew with *The Smell of Christmas* pot pourri, and spend Christmas with Blanche in her home. Aunt Edna stops me before I can develop my inspired plan: 'Honey, they all live so far away, and they have such busy lives.'

After we hang up I'm still worrying. My two widowed great-aunts, so full of life for so long, are dependent on Edna's daughter-in-law, my Aunt Ruby, also a widow, who now lives in my grandmother's large and decrepit house with its half-acre of verandahs. The house went to Ruby because only close family members know how to navigate safely the mosaic of rotten porch boards.

And it's Ruby who calls me back. She assures me that Aunt Blanche doesn't have Alzheimer's. The plan has always been for her to spend Christmas day at Ruby's, together with Edna and all her grand- and great-grandchildren. It's just that Blanche has decided she wants to spend Christmas at the Holiday Inn. She says it has a promising sound.

December 3, 1998

CLEARING THE CLUTTER

My friend Katie has come for Christmas. She's here rather early this year because 'my present to you may take some time'. The morning after she arrived, a lorry lumbered through the farmyard bearing a monster yellow boat with the name Thetford Skip Hire.

'This is a present?'

'This is the beginning of your new life', she replied, gazing mistily as if the crane was unloading the Statue of Liberty. 'I am going to help you get rid of your clutter. When we've cleared some space, I'll *feng shui* Wyken Hall.'

To be scrupulously honest, when it comes to clutter I have few rivals. In a house of nine bedrooms and a cluster of what estate agents call 'reception rooms', there is not a visible surface. Tables are mere platforms for stuff: books, bowls, *objets trouvés* and *objets perdus*, catalogues, coffee mugs, letters, bills. The back stairs look like the periodicals rooms of the London Library: five steps for Country Life, two steps for *The New Yorker*, two steps for *The Spectator*, *Farming News* and *Country Landowner*. Before you can sit down to read any of these, you must first evacuate a space, remove sweaters, handbags, yo-yos, dog leads, combs, sandwich wrappers. If you are foolish enough to wear urban black, you should brush the *couche* of dog hairs, cat hairs and chicken dandruff from the upholstered bits.

'Some people say Wyken looks lived in,' I murmur.

'This isn't lived in,' snaps Katie, 'this is died in. You're dying here. Clutter causes stagnation in every area of your life. Clutter is stuck energy. It's clogging up your physical, mental, emotional and spiritual energy.'

As she speaks I look down at the row of little wellies. When I was yearning for a baby I would stare longingly at the rows of children's wellies lined up in the entrances of my fecund friends. Collections of Postman Pat wellies, green frog wellies and cherry red wellies symbolised everything I wanted in life. I've tenderly kept every pair of Sam's outgrown wellies.

'These should go to the boot room. Every time you enter the house you are entering the past. You don't look down and see Sam's wellies. You relive the sadness of your childless days.'

Katie says she cannot create 'Sacred Space' for me, that I have to create it for myself. She mercifully avoids phrases such as 'removing the obstacles to the harmonious flow of energy in your living environment'. She just says: 'Chaos, mess, junk.'

Before we begin the House Tour she hands me a little blank notebook with a pen tied to it. Inscribed on page one is a Focus list: I. Things you do not use or love; 2. Things which are untidy or disorganised; 3. Too many things; 4. Anything which is unfinished or broken. Her grimaces begin in the larder: 'Bomb shelter mentality.' She's nicer about the kitchen: 'The *Cider with Rosie* look.' She's more alarmed when she sees Sam's room: 'When children feel happy, loved and secure, they don't crave lots of things.' We gaze at Sam's collection of used cartridges, Virgin Cola cans, arrowheads and baseball caps. I can hear her thinking that Sam is acting out his mother's unconscious mind but she says gently, 'He has to make his own decisions. This is important stuff.'

By the time you read this, the skip will be full. Passageways and stairways that 'obstruct the flow of life-bringing energy through the house' have been cleared. The Nordic Health Rider, so useful for hanging clothes on, is no longer in the marital bedroom. All my Christmas shopping has been accomplished without ever leaving the house. The Hempel hotel it is not, but peace and order is magically creeping into Wyken. Of course, some piles have simply been relocated. The Baby Wellie Museum now occupies the rarely used front porch, perched on a set of distinguished plinths: three whole years of COUNTRY LIFE.

December 17, 1998

347

TAP ROOTS

ALL the world can be divided into two basic categories: the natural world and the artificial world. This divide is more poetically known as Nature and Art. When you live in the country, Nature quickly gets the upper hand. First, it surrounds you, then it overcomes you. You may read about the Cézanne exhibition (Art) at the Tate, but what you watch are the crops coming in. You hear about the Millennium Dome (Art?), but your architectural nirvana is the twinkling of lights on the sugar beet harvester at dusk, a North Sea oil platform gliding through a beet field that's bigger than the seventh *arrondissement*.

Although I could write a treatise on the art of chicken massage, speak fluently the ancient language of llamas and never take for granted the miracle that converts grape juice into wine, the truth is, I am not exactly what you'd call a nature lover. When I saw Alan Bennett's play *The Old Country* in the late Seventies, I was the only member of the audience who fully appreciated the line drawled by the English woman as she surveyed the woods behind the dacha of the English defector: 'All this *unnecessary* countryside'.

Of course, Bennett's character was speaking a decade before the epidemic of ticky-tacky houses, gas stations, agribusiness farming, supermarkets and business parks that has sucked up every scrap of unnecessary countryside. But in my heart I share the urbane bluntness of the writer Fran Lebowitz who said: 'I am not the type who wants to go back to the land. I am the type who wants to go back to the hotel.' It's been 12 years since I came back to the land, 12 years in which my Saturdays have been drowned out by the sound of gunfire in the fur and feather wars or by the relentless roar of the grain dryer, known around here as the Suffolk mistral. Twelve years since I spent a leisurely Saturday morning at Portobello Road, followed by an Indian meal at Khan's, showing off my flea market treasures to the waiters, reading *The* (original) *Spectator* and drinking Kingfisher beer while waiting for the butter chicken.

Admittedly, life in the country is not the isolating experience that it was in my childhood. In those days we were 18 miles from the nearest cinema and the closest thing we had to a restaurant was Doe's hot tamales which we brought home wrapped in the *Delta Democrat Times*. Now I can drive two miles to the paper shop in Ixworth and rent the latest video. I can watch Nicole Kidman

349

in *Portrait of a Lady* while I eat Marks & Spencer chicken tikka.

So, did I exaggerate my country roots and rural passion in order to capture the heart of my husband? Yes, dear reader, I did. As we walked through newly coppiced ancient woodland I never complained: 'My God, this looks like the rape of the forest.' On car journeys I meekly listened to his RSPB tapes of birdsong, although I was dying for Nina Simone singing *Lilac Wine*. When my beloved breathed deeply and praised the smell of the countryside after a long, soaking rain, I breathed deeply and thought of spaghettini with fresh pesto.

But, unlike the maiden who assumes a persona that wears away as soon as the slender band of gold is placed on her finger, I have been steadfast. I did not vow to thee my country life, but I've been anchored by the heavy land that is a boon to root crops. While my husband has continued to enjoy the urban joys of Brooks's, Pratts and Starbucks, my clubs have been the CLA, the NFU and Nescafé in the farm workshop with the men. I have surrendered the serenity of the black taxi for the rarer pleasure of the vineyard Fergie. In the debate of Nature versus Art – ice versus ice cubes, the sun versus the microwave, nuts and leaves versus pesto – I still believe that Art has a lot going for it. But now I am far from the madding crowd that craves windfall profits. My roots are in the ham-bony world of cabbages and windfalls. In the currency of the day, I guess you could say that Nature and I have bonded. I've acquired an enduring sense of time and place. It could be worse.

December 10, 1998